TEACHING ENGLISH TO SPEAKERS
OF OTHER LANGUAGES

"This volume, by a highly experienced and well-known author in the field of ELT, takes readers directly into classroom contexts around the world, and asks them to reflect on the teaching practices and the theoretical principles underpinning them, and to engage in questions and discussions that occupy many teachers in their own teaching contexts."

—**Anne Burns**, UNSW, Australia

". . . a fresh look at the craft of TESOL, ideally aimed at the novice teacher. In an interactive approach, Nunan shares theory and engages readers to reflect on both vignettes and their own experiences to better consolidate their understanding of the key concepts of the discipline."

—**Ken Beatty**, Anaheim University, USA

David Nunan's dynamic learner-centered teaching style has informed and inspired countless TESOL educators around the world. In this fresh, straightforward introduction to teaching English to speakers of other languages he presents teaching techniques and procedures along with the underlying theory and principles.

Complex theories and research studies are explained in a clear and comprehensible, yet non-trivial, manner. Practical examples of how to develop teaching materials and tasks from sound principles provide rich illustrations of theoretical constructs. The content is presented through a lively variety of different textual genres including classroom vignettes showing language teaching in action, question and answer sessions, and opportunities to 'eavesdrop' on small group discussions among teachers and teachers in preparation. Readers get involved through engaging, interactive pedagogical features, and opportunities for reflection and personal application. Key topics are covered in twelve concise chapters: Language Teaching Methodology, Learner-Centered Language Teaching, Listening, Speaking, Reading, Writing, Pronunciation, Vocabulary, Grammar, Discourse, Learning Styles and Strategies, and Assessment. Each chapter follows the same format so that readers know what to expect as they work through the text. Key terms are defined in a Glossary at the end of the book. David Nunan's own reflections and commentaries throughout enrich the direct, personal style of the text. This text is ideally suited for teacher preparation courses and for practicing teachers in a wide range of language teaching contexts around the world.

David Nunan is President Emeritus at Anaheim University in California and Professor Emeritus in Applied Linguistics at the University of Hong Kong. He has published over thirty academic books on second language curriculum design, development and evaluation, teacher education, and research and presented many refereed talks and workshops in North America, the Asia-Pacific region, Europe, and Latin America. As a language teacher, teacher educator, researcher, and consultant he has worked in the Asia-Pacific region, Europe, North America, and the Middle East.

TEACHING ENGLISH TO SPEAKERS OF OTHER LANGUAGES

An Introduction

David Nunan

Routledge
Taylor & Francis Group

NEW YORK AND LONDON

First published 2015
by Routledge
711 Third Avenue, New York, NY 10017

and by Routledge
2 Park Square, Milton Park, Abingdon, Oxon OX14 4RN

Routledge is an imprint of the Taylor & Francis Group, an informa business

Library of Congress Cataloging-in-Publication Data
Nunan, David.
    Teaching english to speakers of other languages : an introduction / David
Nunan.
        pages cm
    Includes bibliographical references and index.
    1. English language—Study and teaching—Foreign speakers.   2. Test of
English as a Foreign Language—Evaluation.   3. English language—Ability
testing.   I. Title.
    PE1128.A2N88 2015
    428.0071—dc23
    2014032635

ISBN: 978-1-138-82466-9 (hbk)
ISBN: 978-1-138-82467-6 (pbk)
ISBN: 978-1-315-74055-3 (ebk)

Typeset in Bembo
by Apex CoVantage, LLC

Printed and bound in the United States of America by
Edwards Brothers Malloy on sustainably sourced paper

CONTENTS

INTRODUCTION

This book is an introduction to TESOL – Teaching English to Speakers of Other Languages. I have written it to be accessible to readers who are new to the field, but also hope that it will provide insights for those who have had some experience as TESOL students and teachers.

Before embarking on our journey, I want to discuss briefly what TESOL means and what it includes. TESOL stands for Teaching English to Speakers of Other Languages. TESOL encompasses many other acronyms. For instance, if you are teaching or plan to teach English in an English speaking country, this is an ESL (English as a Second Language) context. If you are teaching in a country whose first language is not English, then you are teaching in an EFL (English as a Foreign Language) context. Sometimes you will also hear the acronym TEAL, which means Teaching English as an Additional Language. Within both ESL and EFL contexts, there are specialized areas, such as ESP (English for Specific Purposes), EAP (English for Academic Purposes), EOP (English for Occupational Purposes), and so on. Some of these terms, and the concepts buried within them such as 'other' and 'foreign,' have become controversial, as I briefly touch on below. I have glossed them here because, if you are new to the field, you will inevitably come across them, and you need to know what they mean.

This textbook is designed to be applicable to a wide range of language teaching contexts. Whether you are currently teaching or preparing to teach, I encourage you to think about these different contexts and the many different purposes that students may have for learning the language.

The TESOL Association was formed fifty years ago. Over these fifty years, massive changes in our understanding of the nature of language and the nature of learning have taken place. There have also been enormous changes in the place of English in the world, and how it is taught and used around the world. In the 1960s, the native speaker of English was the 'norm,' and it was to this 'norm' that second and foreign language learners aspired. (Whose norm, and which norms, were rarely questioned.) Ownership of English was often attributed to England. These days, there are more second language speakers than first language speakers (Graddol, 1996, 2006). Following its emergence as the preeminent global language, first language speakers of English are no longer in a position to claim ownership. There has been a radical transformation in who uses the language, in what contexts, and for what purposes, and the language itself is in a constant state of change.

> The spread of a natural human language across the countries and regions of the planet has resulted in variation as a consequence of nativization and acculturation of the language in various communities . . . These processes have affected the grammatical structure and the use of language according to local needs and conventions . . . Use of English in various contexts manifests in various genres . . . all the resources of multilingual and multicultural contexts are now part of the heritage of world Englishes.
>
> *(Kachru and Smith, 2008: 177)*

With the emergence of English as a global language, traditional TESOL concepts and practices have been challenged. I will go into these concepts and practices in the body of the book. In an illuminating article, Lin *et al.* (2002) tell their own stories of learning, using and teaching English in a range of language contexts. They use their stories to challenge the notion that English is created in London (or New York) and exported to the world. They question the 'other' in TESOL, and propose an alternative acronym – TEGCOM: Teaching English for Global Communication. Many other books and articles as well challenge the 'native' versus 'other' speaker dichotomy, and argue that we need to rethink TESOL and acknowledge a diversity of voices and practices (see, for example, Shin, 2006). These perspectives inform the book in a number of ways. For example, a key principle in the first chapter is the notion that teachers should 'evolve' their own methodology that is sensitive to and consistent with their own teaching style and in tune with their own local context. Also, the central thread of learner-centeredness running through the book places learner diversity at the center of the language curriculum.

How This Book Is Structured

Each chapter follows a similar structure:

- Each chapter begins with a list of chapter *Goals* and an *Introduction* to the topic at hand.
- Next is a classroom *Vignette*. Vignettes are portraits or snapshots. The vignettes in this book are classroom narratives showing part of a lesson in action. Each

is intended to illustrate a key aspect of the theme of the chapter. At the end of the vignette, you will find some of my own observations on the classroom narrative that I found interesting.

- The vignette is followed by an *Issue in Focus* section. Here I select and comment on an issue that is particularly pertinent to the topic of the chapter. For example, in Chapter 1, which introduces the topic of language teaching methodology, I focus on the 'methods debate' which preoccupied language teaching methodologists for many years.
- Next I identify and discuss a number of *Key Principles* underpinning the topic of the chapter.
- The two sections that follow – *What Teachers Want to Know* and *Small Group Discussion* – also focus on key issues relating to the topic of the chapter. *What Teachers Want to Know* takes the form of an FAQ between teachers and teachers in preparation and a teacher educator. The *Small Group Discussion* section takes the form of an online discussion group with teachers taking part in a TESOL program, where a thread is initiated by the instructor, and participants then provide interactive posts to the discussion site.
- Each chapter includes *Reflect* and *Task* textboxes.
- At the end of each chapter is a *Summary*, suggestions for *Further Reading*, and *References*.
- Throughout the textbook, you will be introduced to key terms and concepts. Brief definitions and descriptions of the terms are provided in the *Glossary* at the end of this book.

References

Graddol, D. (1996) *The Future of English*. London: The British Council.

Graddol, D. (2006) *English Next*. London: The British Council.

Kachru, Y. and L. Smith (2008) *Cultures, Contexts, and World Englishes*. New York: Routledge.

Lin, A., W. Wang, N. Akamatsu, and M. Raizi (2002) Appropriating English, expanding identities, and re-visioning the field: From TESOL to teaching English for globalized communication (TEGCOM). *Journal of Language, Identity & Education*, I, 4, 295–316.

Shin, H. (2006) Rethinking TESOL: From a SOL's perspective: Indigenous epistemology and decolonizing praxis in TESOL. *Critical Inquiry in Language Studies*, 3, 3-2, 147–167.

1
LANGUAGE TEACHING METHODOLOGY

Goals

At the end of this chapter you should be able to:

- define the following key terms – curriculum, syllabus, methodology, evaluation, audiolingualism, communicative language teaching, task-based language teaching, grammar-translation, structural linguistics
- describe the 'eclectic' method in which a teacher combines elements of two or more teaching methods or approaches
- set out the essential issues underpinning the methods debate
- articulate three key principles that guide your own approach to language teaching methodology
- say how communicative language teaching and task-based language teaching are related
- describe the three-part instructional cycle of pre-task, task, and follow-up

Introduction

The main topic of this chapter is language teaching methodology, which has to do with methods, techniques, and procedures for teaching and learning in the classroom. This will provide a framework for chapters to come on teaching listening, speaking, reading, writing, pronunciation, vocabulary, and grammar.

Methodology fits into the larger picture of curriculum development. There are three subcomponents to curriculum development: syllabus design, methodology, and evaluation. All of these components should be in harmony with one another: methodology should be tailored to the syllabus, and evaluation/assessment should

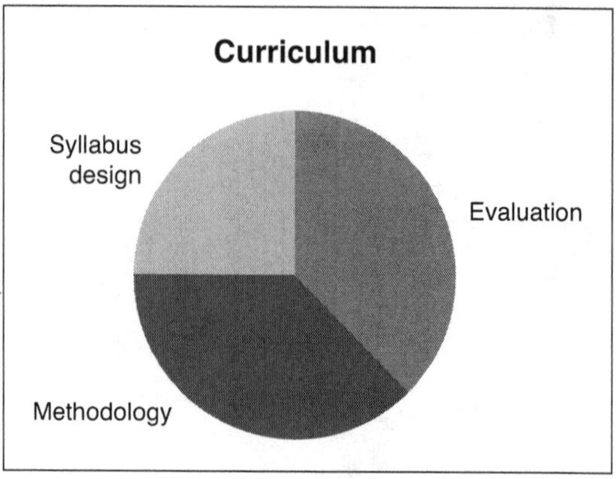

FIGURE 1.1 The three components of the curriculum 'pie'

be focused on what has been taught. (In too many educational systems, what is taught is determined by what is to be assessed.)

Syllabus design focuses on content, which deals not only with what we should teach, but also the order in which the content is taught and the reasons for teaching this content to our learners.

According to Richards *et al.* (1987), methodology is "The study of the practices and procedures used in teaching, and the principles and beliefs that underlie them." Unlike syllabus design, which focuses on content, methodology focuses on classroom techniques and procedures and principles for sequencing these.

Assessment is concerned with how well our learners have done, while evaluation is much broader and is concerned with how well our program or course has served the learners. The relationship between evaluation and assessment is discussed, in some detail, in Chapter 12.

Vignette

As you read the following vignette, try to picture the classroom in your imagination.

The teacher stands in front of the class. She is a young Canadian woman who has been in Tokyo for almost a year. Although she is relatively inexperienced, she has an air of confidence. There are twelve students in the class. They are all young adults who are taking an evening EFL (English as a Foreign Language) class. This is the third class of the semester, and the students and the teacher are beginning to get used to each other. Her students have a pretty good idea of what to expect as the teacher signals that the class is about to begin.

"All right, class, time to get started" she says. "Last class we learned the questions and answers for talking about things we own. 'Is this your pen? Yes, it is. No it isn't. Are these your books? Yes, they are. No, they aren't.' OK? So, let's see if you remember how to do this. *Is this your pen?* Repeat."

The class intones, "Is this your pen?"

"Pencil," says the teacher.

"Is this your pencil?"

"Books."

Most students say, "Are these your books?" However, the teacher hears several of them say, "Is this your books?"

She claps her hands and says loudly "Are these your books? Are these your books? Are these your books? Again! . . . *books*."

"Are these your books?" the students say in unison.

"Good! Great! . . . *those*."

"Are those your books?" say the students.

"Excellent! . . . *her*."

"Are those her book?"

"Book?" queries the teacher.

"Books, books," say several of the students emphasizing the 's' on the end of the verb.

"*Your*"

"Are those your books?"

The teacher beams. "Perfect!" she says. The students smile shyly.

"Now," says the teacher, "Now we'll see how well you can *really* use this language." She passes around a brown velvet bag and instructs the students to put a small, personal object into the bag – a pen, a ring, a pair of earrings. Then, she instructs the students to stand up. She passes the bag around a second time, and tells the students to remove an object. "Make sure it isn't the one that you put in!" she says, and laughs.

When each student has an object or objects that is not his or her own, she makes them stand up and find the owner of the object by asking "Is this your . . .?" or "Are these your . . .?" She repeats the procedure several times, circulating with the students, correcting pronunciation and grammar, until she is satisfied that they are fluent and confident in using the structure.

REFLECT

A. What 3 things did you notice in the vignette? Write them down in note form.

1. _____

2. _____

3. _____

B. Write down 3–5 questions you would like to ask the teacher about the lesson.

My Observations on the Vignette

1. The teacher begins the lesson with a classic audiolingual drill. This is the way that I was trained to teach languages back in the early 1970s. Despite her relative inexperience, the young teacher has confidence because the rigid set of procedures laid out in the audiolingual methodology gives her control of the classroom.

2. The teacher is active. She encourages the students with positive feedback, but also gives gentle correction when they make mistakes. She praises the students without being patronizing. This appears to create a positive classroom environment.

3. In the second phase of the lesson, the teacher uses a technique from communicative language teaching (CLT)/task-based language teaching (TBLT). In my 2004 book on task-based language teaching I called this kind of classroom procedure a "communicative activity" (Nunan, 2004). It is partly a traditional grammar exercise (the students are practicing the grammar structure for the lesson "Is this your/Are these your . . .?), but it has an aspect of genuine communication. The student asking the question doesn't know the answer prior to hearing the response from the person who is answering it.

Issue in Focus: The 'Methods' Debate

For much of its history, the language teaching profession has been obsessed with the search for the one 'best' method of teaching a second or foreign language. This search was based on the belief that, ultimately, there must be a method that would work better than any other for learners everywhere regardless of biographical characteristics such as age, the language they are learning, whether they are learning English as a second language or as a foreign language, and so on. If such a method could be found, it was argued, the language teaching 'problem' would be solved once and for all.

Grammar-Translation

At different historical periods, the profession has favored one particular method over competing methods. The method that held greatest sway is grammar–translation. In fact, this method is still popular in many parts of the world. Focusing on written rather than spoken language, the method, as the name suggests, focuses on the explicit teaching of grammar rules. Learners also spend much time translating from the first to the second language and vice versa. For obvious reasons, the method could only be used in classrooms where the learners shared a common language.

Grammar-translation came in for severe criticism during World War II. The criticism then intensified during the Cold War. The crux of the criticism was that students who had been taught a language through the grammar-translation method knew a great deal about the target language, but couldn't actually use it to communicate. This was particularly true of the spoken language, which is not surprising as learners often had virtually no exposure to the spoken language. This was profoundly unsatisfactory to government bodies that needed soldiers, diplomats, and others who could learn to speak the target language, and who could develop their skills rapidly rather than over the course of years. (I studied Latin in junior high school, and can recall spending hours in the classroom and at home, doing translation exercises with a grammar book and a bilingual dictionary at my elbow.)

Audiolingualism

In his introductory book on language curriculum development, Richards describes audiolingualism as the most popular of all the language teaching methods. In the following quote, he points out that methods such as audiolingualism are underpinned by a theory of language (in this case structural linguistics) and a theory of learning (behaviorism).

> In the United States, in the 1960s, language teaching was under the sway of a powerful method – the *Audiolingual Method*. Stern (1974: 63) describes the period from 1958 to 1966 as the "Golden Age of Audiolingualism." This drew on the work of American Structural Linguistics, which provided the basis for a grammatical syllabus and a teaching approach that drew heavily on the theory of behaviorism. Language learning was thought to depend on habits that could be established by repetition. The linguist Bloomfield (1942: 12) had earlier stated a principle that became a core tenet of audiolingualism: "Language learning is overlearning: anything less is of no use." Teaching techniques made use of repetition of dialogues and pattern practice as a basis for automatization followed by exercises that involved transferring learned patterns to new situations.
>
> (Richards, 2001: 25–26)

In this extract, Richards describes the origins of audiolingualism and summarizes its key principles. Although behaviorism, the psychological theory on which it is based, was largely discredited many years ago, some of the techniques spawned by the method such as various forms of drilling remain popular today. At the beginning stages of learning another language, and also when teaching beginners, I often use some form of drilling, although I always give the drill a communicative cast.

In the 1970s, audiolingualism came in for some severe criticism. Behaviorist psychology was under attack, as was structural linguistics because they did not adequately account for key aspects of language and language learning. This period also coincided with the emergence of 'designer' methods and the rise of communicative language teaching. I used the term 'designer' methods in my 1991 book on language teaching methodology (Nunan, 1991) to capture the essence of a range of methods, such as Suggestopedia and the Silent Way, that appeared in the 1970s and 1980s. These methods provided a clear set of procedures for what teachers should do in the classroom and, like audiolingualism, were based on beliefs about the nature of language and the language learning process.

Communicative Language Teaching

Communicative language teaching was less a method than a broad philosophical approach to language, viewing it not so much as a system of rules but as a tool for communication. The methodological 'realization' of CLT is task-based language teaching (Nunan, 2004, 2014). You will hear a great deal more about CLT in this book, as it remains a key perspective on language teaching. Patsy Duff provides the following introduction to the approach:

> Communicative language teaching (CLT) is an approach to language teach-ing that emphasizes learning a language first and foremost for the purpose of communicating with others. Communication includes finding out about what people did on the weekend . . . or on their last vacation and learning about classmates' interests, activities, preferences and opinions and conveying one's own. It may also involve explaining daily routines to others who want to know about them, discussing current events, writing an email message with some personal news, or telling others about an interesting book or article or Internet video clip.
>
> *(Duff, 2014: 15)*

The search for the one best method has been soundly (and rightly) criticized by language teaching methodologists.

> Foreign language [teaching] . . . has a basic orientation to methods of teach-ing. Unfortunately, the latest bandwagon "methodologies" come into prom-inence without much study or understanding, particularly those that are easiest to immediately apply in the classroom or those that are supported by a particular "guru". Although the concern for method is certainly not a new issue, the current attraction to method stems from the late 1950s, when foreign language teachers were falsely led to believe that there was a method to remedy the "language learning and teaching problem."
>
> *(Richards, 2001: 26)*

While none of the methods from the past should be taken as a 'package deal,' to be rigidly applied to the exclusion of all others, none is entirely without merit, and we can often find techniques from a range of methods, blending these together to serve our purposes and those of our students.

This is what happens in the vignette at the beginning of this chapter. The teacher begins by using a pretty standard form of audiolingual drilling. I say 'standard' because there is no context for the drill, and the focus is purely on manipulating the grammatical form. In the second phase of the lesson, however, she gives the drill a communicative cast as I describe it in my observations on the vignette. She thus blends together activities from two different methods and approaches. This melding of techniques and procedures from more than one method is sometimes described as the 'eclectic method,' which means that it is really no method at all.

Key Principles

In this section, I set out three general principles to guide you as you develop your own classroom approaches, methods, and techniques.

1. Evolve Your Own Personal Methodology

If you are new to teaching, many experienced teachers are likely to tell you, "Oh this is how it should be done." While it would be unwise, even silly, to ignore the advice of the more experienced teacher, whose own insights and wisdom were probably hard-won, ultimately, you need to evolve your own way of teaching: one that suits your personality, is in harmony with your own preferred teaching style, and fits the context and the learners you are teaching. Many years ago, the profession was obsessed with finding the 'one best method,' the secret key that will unlock the door to teaching success. These days, we know that there is no one best method, no single key that will fit all locks. That doesn't mean that you won't occasionally come across teachers who believe that they have found 'the way.' Believe me, they haven't. And your own best way will evolve and change over time as you learn more about the art and science of teaching, as your contexts change, and as the needs of your learners change.

2. Focus on the Learner

This to me is a major key to success, and you will notice me repeating it many times throughout the book. Despite all of our skills and our best intentions, the fact of the matter is that we can't do the learning for our learners. If they are to succeed, then they have to do the hard work. Our job is to 'eazify' the learning for them. This is a word that I once heard a former colleague Chris Candlin use, and it captures the role of the teacher perfectly. The very first learner-centered teacher was the Greek philosopher and educator Socrates, who rejected the notion that the role of the teacher was to pour knowledge into the learner. "Education," he said, "is the lighting of a flame, not the filling of a vessel."

Learners can be involved in their own learning process through a graded sequence of metacognitive tasks that are integrated into the teaching/learning process.

- Make instructional goals clear to the learners.
- Help learners to create their own goals.

- Encourage learners to use their second language outside of the classroom.
- Help learners become more aware of learning processes and strategies.
- Show learners how to identify their own preferred learning styles and strategies.
- Give learners opportunities to make choices between different options in the classroom.
- Teach learners how to create their own learning tasks.
- Provide learners with opportunities to master some aspect of their second language and then teach it to others.
- Create contexts in which learners investigate language and become their own researchers of language.

(I first spelled out how to incorporate these ideas in the classroom in *Second Language Teaching and Learning* [Nunan, 1999]. I will revisit them in subsequent chapters in this book.)

3. Build Instructional Sequences on a Cycle of Pre-Task, Task, and Follow-Up

A cycle may occupy an entire lesson, or the lesson may consist of several cycles. The aim of the pre-task is to set up the learners for the learning task proper. It may focus on developing some essential vocabulary that they will need, it may ask learners to revise a grammar structure, or require them to rehearse a conversation. The task itself may involve several linked tasks or task chains, each of which is interrelated. Finally, there is the follow-up, which may also take various shapes and forms: to get the student to reflect and self-evaluate, to give feedback, to correct errors, and so on. You will get further information and examples on the pre-task, task, follow-up cycle throughout the book.

What Teachers Want to Know

The following section focuses on questions that teachers have about communicative language teaching (CLT)/task-based language teaching (TBLT) and the role of the learner in the communicative classroom.

Question: I've read several articles on communicative language teaching and task-based language teaching. However, I'm not sure what the difference is. Is there a difference?

Response: Communicative language teaching (CLT) is a broad, general, philosophical orientation to language teaching. It developed in the 1970s, when it was realized that language is much more than a system of sounds, words, and grammar rules, and that language learning involves more than mastering these three systems through memorization and habit formation. Teachers also realized that there is a difference between learning and regurgitating grammar rules and being able to use the rules to communicate effectively. This basic insight – that language is a tool for communication rather than sets of rules – led to major challenges to and changes in how teachers went about teaching.

Task-based language teaching (TBLT) is the practical realization of this philosophical shift. Unlike audiolingualism, there is not one single set of procedures that can be labeled TBLT. Rather, it encompasses a family of approaches that are united by two principles: First, meaning is primary, and second, there is a relationship between what learners do in the classroom, and the kinds of things that they will need to do outside the classroom. So the point of departure in designing learning tasks is not to draw up a list of vocabulary and grammar items, but to create an inventory of real-world communication tasks that ask learners to use language, not for its own sake, but to achieve goals that go beyond language, for example, to obtain food and drink, to ask for and give directions, to exchange personal information, and so on.

Question: The aim of communicative language teaching is to give learners the skills to communicate in the real world, outside of the classroom. But I teach in an EFL context. How can I encourage my learners to communicate outside the classroom?

Response: This can be a challenge, but there are many ways to encourage students to communicate outside the classroom. A school I visited recently has an English Only Zone – they call it the EOZ, and when students enter the zone they are only allowed to speak in English. Another idea is to encourage learners to create an EOT (English Only Time) at their home. They choose today's expressions and try to practice or use them during the English Only Time.

The reason why encouraging learners to use the language outside of the classroom is difficult to implement is because we tend to think 'using the second language' means 'speaking' the language. However, you can also practice listening, reading, and writing outside the classroom. When I was teaching in Japan, my students were reluctant to try to speak in English. They might try occasionally when meeting foreigners, but that was fairly rare. So one day, I gave them a chance to write letters to my foreign friends. I told them that my friends are English teachers from all different countries and that they do not know much about Japan. The students worked very hard to make good sentences and structures. They got letters back in English, and some of them still keep in touch with my friends through the Internet. Making a pen pal can be a solution to encourage learners to interact and communicate – it also increases their motivation to learn the language. Also, I suggest watching a lot of movies without subtitles, writing a diary every day, and extensive reading.

Question: How can I encourage learners to be less dependent on the teacher and to take more control of their learning?

Response: The trick is to do this incrementally step-by-step. It is a matter, first of all, of sensitizing learners to the learning process. It's good to be systematic about this, having learning-how-to-learn goals as well as language goals. I do four key things with my learners. I get them thinking about the learning process in general, I encourage them to become more sensitive to the context and environment within which learning takes place, I teach them learning strategies for dealing with listening, speaking, reading, and writing, and I introduce them to strategies for dealing with pronunciation, vocabulary, and grammar. In other words, I get my learners to focus not just on content, but also on processes – strategies for learning. I get them thinking about questions such as, "What sort of learner am I?" "Am I a competitive learner or a co-operative learner?" "Do I like learning by having the teacher tell me everything, or do I like trying to figure things out for myself?"

Being aware of strategies for learning and reflecting on the learning process are keys to taking control of one's learning. Strategies are the mental and cognitive procedures learners use in order to acquire new knowledge and skills – not just language, but all learning. All learning tasks are underpinned by at least one strategy. Learners are usually not consciously aware of these strategies. If we can make them aware of the strategies and get them to apply the strategies to their learning, this can make them more effective and independent learners. Some strategies such as memorizing are common and probably familiar to learners, but others such as classifying, or looking for patterns and regularities in the language, are probably less familiar.

TASK

Brainstorm, if possible with 2–3 other students, and come up with a list of ideas for giving learners opportunities for using English out of class.

Small Group Discussion

In this section, I adapted part of an online discussion thread between a teacher and a group of students. In a previous thread, the students had been discussing the basic instructional sequence of pre-task, task, and follow-up.

In this thread, they are discussing ideas for the pre-task phase of the task cycle.

TEACHER: In this thread, I want you to share ideas for the pre-task phase of the task cycle. Tom, you had some interesting ideas about teaching vocabulary a couple of weeks ago. Do you have any ideas for the pre-task phase that involves vocabulary?

TOM: I put a lot of thought into preparing pre-tasks, I feel they set the tone of my lesson and prepare students for what the class is going to be about. They can motivate the students and get them engaged. One pre-task focused on vocabulary for a reading or listening lesson is the WORDLE website (http://www.wordle.net/). This is a website that generates *word clouds* giving prominence to words that appear more frequently in the text you type in. Students like the final word cloud that the site provides and they can print these out as well as look at them online. Word clouds can be used to get students brainstorming what the reading or listening passage is going to be about. I get my students to make predictions about the words and ask them how the words are connected. Word clouds are very adaptable to students of different ages and levels. Try out the website and let me know what you think.

ALICIA: Thanks for sharing this website with us, Tom. I just checked it out. I like the idea of introducing new vocabulary to students via word clouds as a pre-task. This is new to me and I will definitely use it during one of my upcoming classes.

MARCO: I'm interested in vocabulary and learning strategies. I like to use pre-tasks to set up my junior high school students for new vocabulary that they'll meet in their reading text. I've also checked out the WORDLE website and it looks like fun. I'm going to develop a pre-task for my students using the site. Thanks for suggesting it, Tom.

AUDREY: One book that I love working with provides simple pre-task exercises that you can use to engage students in a certain topic. One is a unit about families. The pre-task contains pictures of different families. Students have to decide which one shows the typical family of the future and discuss reasons for their choices. This prepares them for reading the text about families. In a different unit, before listening or reading about real-life stories of good luck and bad luck, students are asked to share personal examples or experiences with good and bad luck. In many cases, there is a picture with the pre-task, and students have to guess what is happening before doing a listening task. For instance, in a unit on celebrities, students look at pictures and decide what they think a celebrity might be famous for prior to reading about heroes and famous people of our times. Basically, most of the pre-tasks are questions, so students can give their input and brainstorm ideas, vocabulary, sometimes even grammar that will be used on a reading or listening passage. I hope you can use these ideas and try them out, they all work really well if you adjust to the books you are currently using.

JAMES: Here are a few pre-tasks which I've found to be very useful. If you try any of them out and find that they work, please give me feedback.

- The first chapter of the textbook I use talks about brands. I like to play the 'brand game' as an ice-breaker to introduce the whole theme. This can easily be found with a Google search. Students have to identify as many brand logos as they can in a set period of time. The student or the group who guesses the most logos wins.

- An alternative to this, for the same chapter, is to look at a picture of a motorcycle with the Harley-Davidson logo, and ask students what is the first thing that pops into their head when I say "Harley-Davidson." What does the name inspire?

- Following this is a listening text where students have to fill in the gaps. The title of the listening text is "Why brands matter." First, ask students if brands matter to them. Afterwards, get them to try and predict what the recording might be about by predicting what the missing words might be.

- Students get an opportunity to role-play a situation where they are having a business meeting. Before pre-teaching the useful language that is presented in the rest of the chapter, I get students on their own to come up with the best ways to ask for and give opinions. We then compare the students' language with that presented in the book.

- Before reading a text entitled "Road rage in the sky," I got students to try and predict what the text might be about. I asked them what "road rage" is and, once they answered the question, I got them to compare incidences of "road rage" which may have happened to them or someone they know.

- Another chapter in this book is on the topic of leadership. With this chapter, I got students to tell me who they thought made an excellent/terrible leader in the last twenty years. In addition to identifying a person, I asked them to give reasons for their choice. I then got them to try and describe the characteristics of what made these leaders good or bad – making generalizations from their particular instances. Finally, I asked them to compare their lists to the list of adjectives presented in the book.

TEACHER: These are all great pre-tasks. There are so many more that you can use of course. You do, however, have to pay attention to the profile of your group and make adaptations and alterations where necessary.

Commentary

As we can see from the discussions above, there really is no limit to the sort of pre-task activities that learners can carry out in relation to vocabulary, or, indeed, any other aspect of language. It is important to keep in mind that the pre-tasks need to closely connect to, and lead in to, the main task. The pre-tasks can help in connecting learners' background knowledge and experiences to the lesson at hand; they can help in arousing interest in the topic; they can help in revising grammatical structures before doing the main task; and, as we have seen above, they can help in pre-teaching vocabulary used or needed for the main task. Another note about pre-tasks is that they provide learners with time to shift their attention to the topic at hand and the lesson to come.

TASK

Review the pre-task suggestions in the small group discussion, and select one for further development. Describe the steps in the pre-task, create appropriate materials, and briefly describe the task proper for which the pre-task serves as preparation.

Summary

Content focus	Language teaching methodology
Vignette	From audiolingual drill to communicative task
Issue in focus	The 'methods' debate
Key principles	1. Evolve your own personal methodology.
	2. Focus on the learner.
	3. Build instructional sequences on a cycle of pre-task, task, and follow-up.
What teachers want to know	English outside the classroom; learner autonomy; CLT versus TBLT
Small group discussion	Preparing pre-tasks

Further Reading

Richards, J. and T. Rodgers (2014) *Approaches and Methods in Language Teaching*. 3rd Edition. Cambridge: Cambridge University Press.

This book is a classic in the field of language teaching. Jack Richards and his co-author, Ted Rodgers, give a chapter-by-chapter account of the most popular methods of the day so that the reader gets a clear picture of the ways in which methods have evolved and morphed as TESOL evolved.

References

Duff, P. (2014) Communicative language teaching. In M. Celce-Murcia, D. Brinton, and M.A. Snow (eds.) *Teaching English as a Second or Foreign Language*. 4th Edition. Boston: National Geographic Learning.

Nunan, D. (1991) *Language Teaching Methodology*. London: Prentice-Hall.

Nunan, D. (1999) *Second Language Teaching and Learning*. Boston: Heinle & Heinle.

Nunan, D. (2004) *Task-based Language Teaching*. Cambridge: Cambridge University Press.

Nunan, D. (2014) Task-based teaching and learning. In M. Celce-Murcia, D. Brinton, and M.A. Snow (eds.) *Teaching English as a Second or Foreign Language*. 4th Edition. Boston: National Geographic Learning.

Richards, J. (2001) *Curriculum Development in Language Teaching*. Cambridge: Cambridge University Press.

Richards, J.C., J. Platt, and H. Weber (1987) *The Longman Dictionary of Applied Linguistics*. London: Longman.

2

LEARNER-CENTERED LANGUAGE TEACHING

Goals

At the end of this chapter you should be able to:

- define the following key terms and say how they are related: learner-centeredness, autonomy, self-direction
- describe four key principles underpinning a learner-centered approach to instruction
- describe the relationship between in-class instruction and out-of-class language learning and use
- say why learning goals are as important as language goals in the learner-centered classroom

Introduction

One concept that has dominated my teaching, almost from the first moment that I stepped into the classroom, is learner-centeredness. Because the concept permeates this book, I thought that I should give it a chapter all to itself, and that the chapter should appear at the beginning of the book. (For a comprehensive treatment of my approach to the concept, see Nunan, 2013.) The concept acknowledges and incorporates into pedagogy the difference and diversity that characterize learners and learning contexts so clearly articulated by Lin *et al.* (2002) and others. (See also Benson and Nunan, 2005.)

The concept of learner-centeredness is not difficult to understand. However, it can be difficult to implement in the classroom. In the following paragraphs, I will paint some verbal pictures of what I understand by learner-centeredness. When I came across the concept early in my own teaching career, it made intuitive sense, and so it was only natural that I sought to weave it into the fabric of my own teaching. As you read on, you will find that the points articulated in the paragraphs are interrelated. Each describes one face of a multifaceted prism.

In a learner-centered classroom, learning experiences are related to learners' own out-of-class experiences.

The American psychologist David Pearson said that learning is a process of building bridges between what we already know and what we need to learn. This is the basis of the experiential approach to education. We begin with the learners' own experiences, with what they already know, and we find ways to 'hook' new learning onto this pre-existing knowledge.

In a learner-centered classroom, learners take responsibility for their own learning.

We tend to think that this is fine for adults, but is not feasible for children. This is not true. The educator Gene Bedley once said that whenever we do something for children that they could do for themselves we are taking away from them an opportunity to learn self-responsibility and independence (Bedley, 1985). In my own work, I have found that children as young as eleven can begin to take control of their own learning.

In a learner-centered classroom, learners are engaged in their own learning.

If they are not engaged, it is unlikely that they will learn. If you spend time in pre-school classrooms (and I strongly recommend that you do, regardless of the age level you teach or plan to teach) it will be easy to see when a child is disengaged. He or she will simply get up and wander away.

In a learner-centered classroom, learners are involved in making decisions about what to learn, how to learn, and how to be assessed.

Teaching and learning are in harmony, and the educational enterprise is a collaborative process between the teacher and the learner. Learners are active participants in their own learning, rather than passive objects to be manipulated.

In a learner-centered classroom, there are two sets of goals: language goals and learning goals.

In a language classroom, of course, we have language goals. Why have learning goals? The answer is that most learners do not come into the classroom with skills and knowledge to make informed decisions about what to learn, how to learn, and how to be assessed. They need to learn these skills, and to be sensitized to their own preferred ways of learning.

In a learner-centered classroom, the strategies underlying the pedagogical tasks in which learners are engaged will be made transparent.

All tasks are underpinned by one or more strategies. Learners are more likely to incorporate these into their language learning if they know what they are and how they can be used.

The ultimate goal of a learner-centered teacher is to make him- or herself redundant. As my colleague Geoff Brindley wrote over thirty years ago:

> One of the fundamental principles underlying the notion of permanent education is that education should develop in individuals the capacity to control their own destiny and that, therefore, the learner should be seen as being at the centre of the educational process. For the teaching institution and the teacher, this means that instructional programmes should be centred around the learners' needs and that learners themselves should exercise their own responsibility in the choice of learning objectives, content and methods as well as in determining the means used to assess their performance.
>
> *(Brindley, 1984: 15)*

Brindley was thinking of adult learners when he made this statement. However, I believe that it is relevant to *all* learners. As I write this book, I am working with a group of ten–eleven-year-olds in Korea. With appropriate guidance and support, these children are able to articulate how they learn best, which kinds of activities they like to engage in, and which they don't. They can also tell you how they go about learning and using language, not just inside the classroom, but outside as well.

Vignette

In this vignette, a group of high-intermediate young adults in an EFL setting are attending the first day of class with a new teacher. The teacher introduces herself and then says, "In the lesson today, I want to find out your ideas about what you want to learn, how you like to learn, and how you want to be assessed. I also want to learn about what you *don't* like. So, I'm going to give you a little survey to do, OK?" She hands a sheaf of papers to the student sitting nearest to her and asks the student to distribute the surveys to the class. "I want you to complete the survey individually. Then, when you have finished, I'll tell you what comes next."

The designated student distributes the following survey to her classmates.

LEARNING PREFERENCES SURVEY

Complete the survey by circling the number that corresponds to your own beliefs about how you like to learn.

Key

1. I don't like this at all
2. I don't like this very much

3.   This is OK
4.   I quite like this
5.   I like this very much

I. Topics

In my English class, I would like to study topics . . .

1.   about me: my feelings, attitudes, beliefs, etc. (1 2 3 4 5)
2.   from my academic subjects: psychology, history, etc. (1 2 3 4 5)
3.   from popular culture: music, films, etc. (1 2 3 4 5)
4.   about current affairs and issues (1 2 3 4 5)
5.   that are controversial: underage drinking, etc. (1 2 3 4 5)

II. Methods

In my English class, I would like to learn by . . .

6.   small group discussions and problem-solving (1 2 3 4 5)
7.   formal language study, e.g. studying from a textbook (1 2 3 4 5)
8.   listening to the teacher (1 2 3 4 5)
9.   watching videos (1 2 3 4 5)
10.   doing individual work (1 2 3 4 5)

III. Language Areas

This semester, I most want to improve my . . .

11.   listening (1 2 3 4 5)
12.   speaking (1 2 3 4 5)
13.   reading (1 2 3 4 5)
14.   writing (1 2 3 4 5)
15.   grammar (1 2 3 4 5)
16.   pronunciation (1 2 3 4 5)

IV. Out of Class

Out of class, I like to . . .

17.   practice in the independent learning center (1 2 3 4 5)
18.   have conversations with native speakers of English (1 2 3 4 5)
19.   practice English online through social media (1 2 3 4 5)
20.   collect examples of interesting/puzzling English (1 2 3 4 5)
21.   watch TV/read newspapers in English (1 2 3 4 5)

V. Assessment

I like to find out how my English is improving by . . .

22. having the teacher assess my written work (1 2 3 4 5)
23. having the teacher correct my mistakes in class (1 2 3 4 5)
24. checking my own progress/correcting my own mistakes (1 2 3 4 5)
25. being corrected by my fellow students (1 2 3 4 5)
26. seeing if I can use the language in real-life situations (1 2 3 4 5)

As they work, the teacher monitors the students. When she sees that they have finished, she calls them to attention and says, "OK. Now I want you to get into groups of three to four, and I want you to compare your answers. See where you agree and where you disagree. And then what I want you to do is to come up with a group survey – I'll give each group a clean survey sheet. You won't all agree on everything, so, what you have to do is to discuss and compromise. Everyone has different ideas to a certain extent, so compromise is important. You understand compromise? Yes? OK, off you go. If you don't know each other, introduce yourselves, and then do the joint survey. And remember, you have to give reasons for your choices."

While the students work, the teacher circulates and intervenes in one group where there seems to be disagreement. When everyone appears to be finished, she gets their attention and carries out a debriefing. Each group has to report their top choice for each of the subcategories on the survey and their least preferred options.

When they get to the last subcategory, on assessment, one student reports that their most preferred option is having the teacher assess their written work. The other students nod in agreement.

"And your least preferred option?" asks the teacher.

"Being corrected by my fellow students," says the student. Again, there is general agreement around the room.

"Why is that?" asks the teacher.

"Because we are all the same. We, are, we all have equal footing. How can my fellow student correct me? We all have the same ability in the language. If I make a mistake, she will make the same mistake. He will make the same mistake."

"But maybe by working together, you can help each other. Four heads are better than one."

The student looks doubtful.

"In this class, I want you all to work together co-operatively. You have seen that there are some things you agree on, and some things you don't agree on, so there are times that we have to compromise. Say I give you an assignment and say that you have to hand it in on Friday. Perhaps you have an assignment from another teacher that is also due on Friday. You can come to me and negotiate. 'Jane, can we have until Monday to hand in your assignment?' And, if it's possible, then I'll say 'Yes.' But you know, there are times when it's good to try out ways of learning that maybe you don't like. Maybe you don't like having conversations out of class with native speakers because you feel shy. But if you try it from time to time, you might see that it has real benefits. So, it's good to expand, to extend the ways that you go about learning. We'll be doing another survey in a couple of weeks to see whether your ideas about language and learning have changed as a result of the learning experiences in class."

REFLECT

A. What 3 things did you notice in the vignette? Write them down in note form.

1. _____
2. _____
3. _____

B. Write down 3–5 questions you would like to ask the teacher about the lesson.

My Observations on the Vignette

1. The teacher sets the agenda clearly in the very first lesson. The students learn that they will be actively involved in making decisions about what they will learn, how they will learn, and how they will be assessed. There is a clear expectation that they should look for opportunities to practice their English outside of the classroom. Class time will be used for active, collaborative learning rather than listening to the teacher. The two key interpretations of 'learner-centeredness' are evident in the vignette. First, learners' attitudes, ideas, and preferences will be taken into account in making curricular decisions. Second, learners will be actively involved in learning through doing.

2. Learners won't necessarily get everything they want. The pedagogical agenda will be negotiated, and there will be times when compromise will be necessary. Teachers have their agendas, and there are many situations in which the teacher knows best, and brings his/her professional skills and knowledge to bear in the learning situation.

3. In the final statement to the class, the teacher makes it clear that during the semester, there will be opportunities for learners to reflect on their learning preferences, and that their ideas are likely to evolve as they think about their own learning processes. Andragogy, the study of adult learning, has had a significant influence on learner-centered language teaching. A study that influenced my own thinking back in the early 1980s was Brundage and MacKeracher (1980).

Issue in Focus: Negotiated Learning

The idea that learners can and should contribute to their own learning by making decisions about what they should learn, how they should learn, and how they should be assessed is controversial. Some teachers feel that the notion calls into question their professional expertise. At a seminar in which I spoke about the virtues of negotiated learning, a teacher asserted that asking learners for advice on what and how to learn was like a doctor asking a patient for advice on what medication to prescribe. This analogy is misguided. As teachers, we are not setting out to cure our learners of the malady of monolingualism. While it is true that we have professional knowledge and expertise on language teaching and learning, ultimately, if learning is to occur, it is the learners themselves who have to do the work. Some learners have clear ideas about what they want to learn and how they want to learn; however, many do not. It's for this reason that we need to begin helping them to take control of their own learning. I will give some ideas on how this can be done in this section.

Resistance to negotiation can also come from learners who feel that it is the teacher's responsibility to make decisions about the what and how of learning. Personally, I've never encountered this problem. In fact, negotiation is a normal part of the teaching learning process. When students ask for an extension on an assignment, they are negotiating. When, in a lesson involving both reading and listening, you ask whether they would like to do the reading or the listening task first, you are negotiating.

I make a modest beginning to the process of sensitizing my students to the central role they must play in their own learning process. How I go about this depends on the age and proficiency level of the students. If I'm dealing with adults, I make the instructional goals of the course clear to the learners in the first lesson. Then, each time I teach a lesson, I make the goals of that lesson clear to the learners. At the end of the lesson, I do a brief review, getting the learners to self-evaluate, on a checklist, the extent to which they have achieved the goals of the lesson. As the course progresses, I get the students to select their own goals from a 'menu' of goal statements. Ultimately, I work toward the point of getting learners to create their own learning goals.

Parallel to this goal-setting exercise, I work on raising students' awareness of learning processes. I make them aware of the strategies underlying the tasks and exercises that we work on in the classroom, and I give them exercises to help them identify their own preferred learning styles and strategies. (This is an important topic, which Chapter 11 is devoted to.) As I've already stated, I have found that children as young as ten and eleven can describe how, for example, they go about learning new vocabulary. This does not mean that they know intuitively the most effective way of learning vocabulary, but raising awareness of how they go about learning new words is a first step toward exploring a range of alternative ways of increasing their vocabulary.

From the very first lesson, I get learners making choices. "Do you want to work in pairs or groups?" "Do you want to do the listening task or the reading task?" Even young learners can make these choices. At the end of a unit of work, I get them to tell me which task they liked best, which they liked least, and why.

At a more advanced level, I get learners to master a skill, technique, or piece of language and then teach this to the other students. For example, students in groups can each have their own reading passage. They master the passage and create reading comprehension questions. They then exchange the passage and the questions with another group. One of my graduate students used a similar technique as part of her dissertation work. Her learners each created a video project which they used to teach the other students in the class.

She reported that:

> The goal of "teaching each other" was a factor of paramount importance. Being asked to present something to another group gave a clear reason for the work, called for greater responsibility to one's own group, and led to increased motivation and greatly improved accuracy. The success of each group's presentation was motivated by the response and feedback of the other group; thus there was a measure of in-built evaluation and a test of how much had been learned. Being an "expert" on a topic noticeably increased self-esteem and getting more confident week-by-week gave [the learners] a feeling of genuine progress.
>
> *(Assinder, 1991: 228)*

Another technique that I have found to be useful is to encourage learners to become researchers of their own language. Learners, regardless of their level of proficiency, can bring samples of language that they encounter out of class into the classroom. These can be new words and phrases, samples of environmental print that they can capture on their cell phones, snippets of conversation, etc. More advanced learners can become communities of ethnographers, "collecting, interpreting, and building a data bank of information about language in their worlds" (Heath, 1992: 53). Although this can be challenging, it is also rewarding. By becoming ethnographers, students come to appreciate that communication, as well as learning, is negotiated.

Key Principles

1. Provide Opportunities for Learners to Reflect on Their Learning Processes

Reflective learning is fundamental to the whole concept of learner-centeredness. It is also a key component of experiential learning. In experiential learning, the learners' immediate experiences form the point of departure for the learning process. They act and then reflect on their learning, and through the act of reflecting, their learning is transformed. Being reflective is not something that comes naturally to all learners, and they therefore need systematic opportunities to think critically about their learning.

On a related point, Benson (2003: 296) notes that learners' choices and decisions ultimately become meaningful through their consequences. He notes that:

> Many teachers feel that direction (by the teacher) is justified because it makes learning more efficient. If students decide things for themselves, they will make mistakes and precious time that could otherwise be spent on learning will be wasted. The argument against this is that mistakes are an opportunity for learning. We know, for example, that linguistic errors in speaking and writing may be a form of hypothesis testing that is important to language acquisition.

2. Give Learners Opportunities to Contribute to Content, Learning Procedures, and Assessment

The teacher can plan in advance opportunities to make choices and decisions, or they can arise spontaneously in the course of a lesson. The choices and decisions can be made at different levels involving not just what and how to learn, but also who to work with.

3. Be Guided by Adult Learning Principles When Working with More Mature Learners

Andragogy, or the study of adult learning, had an important influence on proponents of learner-centered instruction. A study by Brundage and MacKeracher (1980), which sets out principles of adult learning, had a significant influence on my own thinking about learner-centeredness in the early 1980s. Their principles include the notion that adults learn best when they are involved in developing learning objectives for themselves that are congruent with their current and idealized self-concept. They also learn best when the content is personally relevant to past experience or present concerns and the learning process is relevant to life experiences.

4. Incorporate Learner Training into the Curriculum

This is an important point: so important that an entire chapter (Chapter 11) is devoted to it later in the book. I have already mentioned the importance of having twin sets of goals in your curriculum, one set devoted to language and the other set devoted to the learning process and learning how to learn. There are two ways of interpreting the concept of learner-centeredness. On the one hand, the concept relates to the involvement of learners in making decisions and choices about content and procedures. On the other hand, it relates to learners taking an active role in learning through doing. If learners are to make choices, about what they learn and how they learn, they need training in the skills and knowledge that are required to make such decisions. Without such knowledge, it is impossible to make informed decisions. Also, if learners are conditioned to classrooms in which the teacher makes all of the decisions, they may find it strange that they are being asked to make choices and decisions. There may be learner resistance to the idea from learners who believe that it's the teacher's job to make these decisions.

If, as a teacher, you are committed to creating a classroom in which the students learn through doing, then you need to ensure that the learners are aware that they will be expected to learn through active participation in collaborative, small group work. For learners who have come from educational systems in which they were relatively passive recipients of information through whole-class and individual exercises, this new role can be challenging and even threatening. The learners need to understand and appreciate the rationale for the change of roles. This can be achieved through learner training. They get to appreciate the learning strategies and rationale behind the tasks they are being asked to carry out both in and out of class, and can also begin to identify the kinds of strategies that work best for them. For example, do they learn best through seeing or hearing, by tasks that require reading and writing, or those that demand listening and speaking?

What Teachers Want to Know

The focus of this discussion thread is learner autonomy and its relationship to learner-centeredness, along with the related concepts of self-directed learning and individualization.

Question: Can you tell us something about learner autonomy? What does it have to do with learner-centeredness?

Response: What holds the concepts of learner-centeredness and autonomy together is the notion that, ultimately, if someone is going to learn anything, be it a language or anything else, he or she has to do it themselves. As a teacher, you can't do the learning for your learners. An autonomous learner is someone who can make informed choices about what they want to learn and how they want to learn.

Question: But if learners are autonomous, won't that put teachers out of a job?

Response: This is a common misconception. The 'father' of autonomy in language learning, Henri Holec (1981), described autonomy as the ability to take control of one's own learning. Paradoxically, that may involve choosing to give up control to a teacher. When I lived in Bangkok many years ago, I decided to attempt to learn Thai without taking formal instruction. Within a few weeks, I realized that I had bitten off more then I could chew, and that if I wanted to make any serious progress in learning the language, I would need to take lessons. My decision to enroll in a language class was an exercise in autonomy.

I like Benson's definition of autonomy as "the capacity to take charge of, or responsibility for, our own learning" (2001: 47). He goes on to say that:

> control over learning may take a variety of forms in relation to different levels of the learning process. In other words, it is accepted that autonomy is a multidimensional capacity that will take different forms for different individuals, and even for the same individual in different contexts or at different times.

Question: Does this mean that there is a difference between autonomy, self-directed learning, and individualized learning?

Response: Yes, there are differences, although the terms are closely related. Self-directed learning is generally conceived of as learning outside the classroom in situations where the learners are responsible for the planning and execution of their own learning. As already indicated, there are different levels of autonomy, and the autonomous learner may choose classroom instruction, or they may choose the self-directed path – becoming an independent learner outside of the classroom. Individualized learning involves instruction that is tailored to the individual learner, although there may be nothing about the learning that is under the control of the learner. In individualized learning, pedagogical decisions may be under the total control of the teacher.

Question: So, how can we activate autonomy in the classroom?

Response: One practical way is to make it clear on the very first day of the class that the students will be expected to take an active role in, and to make decisions about, their own learning. Benson presents a good example of this from a course taught by Andrew Littlejohn (1983). Littlejohn began the course by getting students to complete a questionnaire on their learning experiences and preferences. The results were summarized, placed on the board, and discussed. As Benson points out, although this activity was teacher-directed, it conveyed an important message: that the students' preferences and opinions would be important in determining learning content and procedures. The next step was for students working in small groups to analyze the grammar textbook they had used in the previous course and to evaluate the difficulty of the grammar topics and tasks using the following textbook evaluation sheet.

Look at each section of each unit that you have been assigned and try to fill in the table below.

Unit/section: _____

What exactly does the section ask you to do?

How difficult is it? 1 2 3 4 5 6 7 8 9 10

very easy   very difficult

Personally:_____ Group average: _____

(Adapted from Littlejohn, 1983)

Again, the task is teacher-directed, but the students are actively involved in evaluating and making decisions about what will be the content focus of their new course.

Awareness-raising activities such as these can be incorporated into the course once it has begun. For example, in my work with young learners in Korea, at the end of a unit, I get the learners in small groups to evaluate the unit by looking through it and selecting the task that they most enjoyed and say why, and the task that they least enjoyed and say why. They are permitted to carry out this task in Korean, but the reporting back to the class must be in English. In one particular unit, the majority of groups selected a vocabulary task as the most enjoyable. When asked why, they said that vocabulary was essential for language learning. This led on to a discussion of what strategies they used to learn vocabulary. It was clear from their responses that these young learners were capable of thinking about the learning process and articulating their ideas and opinions.

TASK

Select a textbook that you have used or that you might be interested in using and design a learner evaluation questionnaire, either for the book as a whole, or for one of the units in the book.

The questionnaire can focus on one or all of the following:

- task difficulty
- task interest
- task enjoyment
- task usefulness
- task relevance to learners' current needs.

Small Group Discussion

The teacher introduces this discussion thread by stressing the importance of making links between classroom language learning and activating language outside the classroom. She begins by getting the teachers to reflect on their own second language learning experiences outside of the classroom.

TEACHER: We've spent a lot of time this week talking about learner-centeredness, and we've looked at ways of implementing learner-centeredness inside the classroom. But we also need to prepare our learners for learning and using language outside the classroom. After all, that's where learners spend most of their time. Encouraging learners to practice in the world outside of our classrooms is an important aspect of the whole learner-centered philosophy. As well as being teachers, you're also all successful second language learners. So I want you to think of some of the ways that you developed your second language skills outside of the classroom. Who'd like to share their experiences?

JULIE: I'd be happy to get this thread started. When I was beginning to learn Italian, I got quite frustrated with my teacher. There was nothing learner-centered about her approach. In fact, she was one of those teachers who had that "I'm the doctor and I know what's best for you" attitude.

KIM: I had a teacher like that when I was learning Chinese. What did you do about it, Julie?

JULIE: I realized that I needed to supplement, if not replace, my in-class learning with my own ways of learning outside the classroom. I could have found ways on the Internet, but I love to read and I came across an article on extensive reading and its benefits for language development. It was making an argument for the benefits of extensive reading for first language readers, but I thought, "Maybe this could work for me too." At first, I got a book of short stories. It was one of those bilingual editions with the Italian on one page and English on the facing page.

TOMOKO: It sounds interesting. How did it work out?

JULIE: Well, the problem was that the original stories were way too difficult. They were written for native speakers of Italian, after all. It would take me like an hour to read a couple of paragraphs with a bilingual dictionary, and then I'd get interested in the story and read the English translation. That didn't do much for my Italian, I can tell you! So, then, I thought, "I need to get reading material that's closer to my level." I wrote to a friend in Rome and asked her to send me some kids' fairy stories – I mean for really little kids. Soon a bunch of books arrived – 'The Three Little Pigs,' 'Cinderella,' 'Goldilocks.' They were great. I knew the stories, so I had the background knowledge, and I could focus on the way that the language worked. Even the title of 'The Three Little Pigs' – 'I tre porcellini' – taught me useful grammar.

Then I discovered that a lot of these stories were available on the Internet, and I ended up reading dozens of kids' storybooks in Italian.

TOMOKO: Do you still do it?

JULIE: I do. But now, I'm up to reading books for young teenagers!

TEACHER: Kim, how did you supplement your in-class learning of Chinese?

KIM: I came across this email exchange program.

JULIE: Email exchange program? How does that work?

KIM: It's a web-based program called email tandem learning that matches two people up who are learning each other's language. So, I was linked up with a Chinese woman in Shanghai who was learning English. We emailed each other on topics of mutual interest. She wrote to me in English and I wrote to her in Chinese. We talked about things such as school life, cooking, and fashion. During the exchanges, we asked each other questions, asked for clarification and that sort of thing. It was just like having a conversation except that it was through the Internet, and it was text chat.

JULIE: So it wasn't a 'real' voice conversation. Why didn't you just get on Skype?

KIM: Well, the good thing about text chat was that we could comment on each other's language. She would say "I thought what you had to say about your kid's school system was interesting. Here's how we would say it in Chinese." And she would correct what I had written. I would give her similar feedback on her English. So the benefit of email over say Skype was that it 'captured' the conversation, and we could study each other's contributions. What I found most valuable was not only the feedback I got on my Chinese, but I also got a lot of cultural information that I wouldn't have gotten from a textbook. I also kept a journal of the experience and the things I learned from it. I'd review the journal from time to time and it gave me a lot of insights, not only into Chinese language and culture, but also into my own learning processes.

TEACHER: So you really took control of your own learning.

KIM: I did.

TEACHER: Tomoko, what was your experience?

TOMOKO: Well, I was born and grew up in Hawaii – my parents moved there from Osaka before I was born. I had a bit of exposure to Japanese at home, but it was pretty basic. English was really my first language. When I graduated from university, I decided to study Japanese on my own. I had a whole bunch of self-study books, and I found a conversation partner. It wasn't an online learning experience like Kim's, but face-to-face. My partner was a native speaker of Japanese who was studying English in the Los Angeles area. We would meet for coffee every couple of weeks and switch between English and Japanese every fifteen minutes or so. Then I decided to go and live in Japan for a few months with an American friend. At first it was really difficult. Because I look Japanese, people thought I was Japanese, they would speak to me as though I was a native speaker of Japanese, so there was a cultural barrier that I had to overcome. But I went out of my way to meet people and to interact with them. My friend also had a tough time at first, although for different reasons. She found it intimidating and difficult to have conversations with people, so she set herself little assignments.

KIM: Can you give us some examples?

TOMOKO: Well, she would go to festivals, and other public events and would talk to people about the event. She'd ask things like why the event was important, what its cultural significance was, and so on. On the street, she'd ask people for directions to the bank or a certain restaurant – that sort of thing, even though she knew where these places were. She had about ten types of contact assignment that gave her a legitimate excuse to interact with native speakers. Without these, she said she'd probably just sit in her room and study Japanese the way she would at home.

Commentary

In this discussion thread, students talk about their own techniques for practicing their second language outside the classroom. The thread illustrates the rich contexts and opportunities for practicing languages in different parts of the world. One student used fairy tales for children. Another took part in an email tandem exchange. A third describes a conversation exchange technique, along with contact tasks with native speakers when on an exchange program.

TASK

Brainstorm and come up with ways of learning language out of class. Think about:

Where (at home, in public places such as museums)
Mode (speaking or writing; face-to-face or online)
Skill (listening, speaking, reading, writing)
Media (print – book, newspaper; audio – radio; visual – television, video; Internet).

Summary

Content focus	Learner-centered language teaching
Vignette	Learner preferences
Issue in focus	Negotiated learning

Key principles	1. Provide opportunities for learners to reflect on their learning processes.
	2. Give learners opportunities to contribute to content, learning procedures, and assessment.
	3. When working with more mature learners, be guided by adult learning principles.
	4. Incorporate learner training into the curriculum.
What teachers want to know	Autonomy and self-direction
Small group discussion	Out-of-class learning

Further Reading

Benson, P. (2001) *Teaching and Researching Autonomy in Language Learning*. London: Longman.

This book provides a comprehensive introduction to the theory, research, and practice of learner autonomy.

References

Assinder, W. (1991) Peer teaching, peer learning; one model. *ELT Journal*, 45, 3, 218–229.

Bedley, G. (1985) *The Big R: Responsibility. Encouraging and Cultivating Responsible Behavior*. Irvine, CA: People-Wise Publications.

Benson, P. (2001) *Teaching and Researching Autonomy in Language Learning*. London: Longman.

Benson, P. (2003) Learner autonomy in the classroom. In D. Nunan (ed.) *Practical English Language Teaching*. New York: McGraw-Hill.

Benson, P. and D. Nunan (eds.) (2005) *Learners' Stories: Difference and Diversity in Language Learning*. Cambridge: Cambridge University Press.

Brindley, G. (1984) *Needs Analysis and Objective Setting in the Adult Migrant Education Program*. Sydney: Adult Migrant Education Service.

Brundage, D.H. and H. MacKeracher (1980) *Adult Learning Principles and Their Application in Program Planning*. Toronto: Ontario Institute for Studies in Education.

Heath, S.B. (1992) Literacy skills or literate skills? Considerations for ESL/EFL learners. In D. Nunan (ed.) *Collaborative Language Learning and Teaching*. Cambridge: Cambridge University Press.

Holec, H. (1981) *Autonomy in Foreign Language Learning*. Oxford: Pergamon.

Lin, A., W. Wang, N. Akamatsu, and M. Raizi (2002) Appropriating English, expanding identities, and re-visioning the field: From TESOL to teaching English for globalized communication (TEGCOM). *Journal of Language, Identity & Education*, I, 4, 295–316.

Littlejohn, A. (1983) Increasing learner involvement in course management. *TESOL Quarterly*, 17, 4, 595–608.

Nunan, D. (2013) *Learner-Centered English Language Education: The Selected Works of David Nunan*. New York: Routledge.

3

LISTENING

Goals

At the end of this chapter you should be able to:

- define the following key terms: comprehensible input, background knowledge, scaffolding
- differentiate between receptive and productive language skills
- identify the learning strategies of classifying and listening for key words
- describe the difference between top-down and bottom-up listening
- discuss four key principles for teaching listening

Introduction

Some years ago at a conference, I was asked to describe the place of listening in second language learning. My reply, which seemed somewhat glib at the time, was that listening is the gasoline in the engine of second language acquisition. Later, when I reflected on my answer, I thought that it was reasonably accurate. The engine in a car doesn't run without gasoline (or, these days, electricity or some other form of power). It simply won't happen. Without access to comprehensible input in the form of aural or written messages, a second language won't happen.

You may sometimes hear about the 'four skills' approach to language learning. In this context, 'skills' refers to listening, speaking, reading, and writing. Listening and reading are receptive skills. Through them we receive target language input. Speaking and writing are productive skills. Of the four listening is fundamental. It is even more important than reading, although, as I argue in Chapter 5, reading is also an extremely important, and sometimes overlooked, skill. The Canadian educator and applied linguist David Mendelsohn once described listening as the 'Cinderella Skill.' He wrote, "despite a gradually increasing acceptance of the importance of listening comprehension for second language learners, the teaching of listening comprehension remains a somewhat neglected and poorly taught aspect of English in many ESL programs – the 'Cinderella' skill of ESL" (1994: 9).

While listening and reading provide input, they are quite different. When we listen, we have to snatch sounds from the air before they evaporate. With reading, we can pause, ponder, and reread.

For many second language learners, listening is more fundamental than reading in the initial stages of learning because they may not understand the written script. As I mentioned in the previous chapter, years ago, I lived in Thailand. Because I was living in a neighborhood of Bangkok where not a single person understood or spoke English, I had to pick up Thai pretty quickly. I couldn't do this by reading because the Thai script was totally different from the Roman alphabet. To gain access to the language, I had to rely exclusively on the sounds that surrounded me. This was quite a challenge, because I am a visual learner: I learn better by seeing rather than hearing. (For comprehensive book-length treatments of listening in second language learning, see Field [2008] and Rost [2011].)

Vignette

This class takes place in an immigrant language center in Australia. The class consists of a group of adult immigrants of different ages and nationalities. It's the beginning of the class, and the students sit in a large semi-circle chatting to each other until the teacher calls them to order by saying, "Now we're going to listen to the news, and I'm going to hand out a worksheet to you all, and we're going to do, as we have done before. Just listen and decide which category the news item you hear falls into. So, I'll pass these around, and you just read the instructions."

The teacher then distributes the following worksheet.

LISTENING TASK

Put a tick next to the category or categories each news item belongs to.

Categories

Political/Government

Overseas

Disaster/Accident

Sports

Art/Culture

Religion

Economics

Health

Education

Defense/Military

Judiciary

Once all students have a copy of the worksheet, she says, "I'll just play the main titles, or headlines, and I want you just to get a general idea of the topics. Right? So, you don't have to tick the boxes in now, you can just listen." She then plays the extract, which has been recorded from a radio news bulletin.

> *This is ABC national news read by Tony Jones. Here are the headlines. Overseas, a shake-up in the currency and stock markets. More fighting in the Middle East, and in Moscow, the death of superspy Reg Smith. On the local scene, financial cutting expected at today's state government leaders' conference. Other items in the news are student demonstrations, the cost of IVF babies, and aboriginal cricketers. The news in detail after this break.*

The teacher pauses the broadcast and turns to a student sitting on her left. She says, "What're you going to do, Irene?" She points to the whiteboard on which she has written some of the news categories. "Next time you listen, what will you be doing?"

"I'm going to tick what categories they go in. Different items," replies Irene.

"Good." The teacher plays the headlines again. The students listen a second time and tick the different categories on the handout as they do so.

"Now," says the teacher, "just before we listen for the third time, check with a partner what they've . . . how many they've ticked on theirs and see if you've got the same or if you can remember any of the items."

The students work in small groups comparing their handouts. The teacher gives them three or four minutes to complete this phase of the lesson and then draws their attention to the front of the class. "So this time listen just to confirm whether what you heard was accurate or not," she says, and then plays the first part of the broadcast again.

This is ABC national news read by Tony Jones. Here are the headlines. Overseas, a shake-up in the currency and stock markets.

"Right, what did you . . . would you tick for that?"

"Overseas. Business," say several of the students.

"Overseas, and . . .?"

"Business . . . business . . . business and economical."

"Business and . . . where is it?" The teacher points to the words on the board.

"Economic," says a student.

"Economics, because the reader says the word . . . which word gave you that clue? Beginning with 'C'?"

"Stock market," says a student.

The teacher nods. "Stock market. And . . .?"

"Currency."

"Currency. Good. OK, so, two categories there – overseas and economics. Let's listen to the next one."

The students listen to the next few items, completing them with few problems until they reach the last item. The teacher says, "Medical . . . and . . .?"

"And, er, economics," says a student.

"And economics, yes, because they're talking about the cost of it. Good." She then plays the last item in the bulletin.

. . . and aboriginal cricketers . . .

"And . . . Shaheed?"

There is some confusion. Shaheed, the nominated student, confers with a number of other students.

"What would you put it under?" asks the teacher.

"Er, political . . . political . . . political," says Shaheed.

"Judicial," says another student.

"What were the two words you heard?"

"Culture, culture."

"I'll just play that bit again."

She replays the item, and this time several of the students get it. "Aboriginal cricketers. Aboriginal cricket. Sport," they call out.

"You changed your minds and decided . . .?"

"Sport. Sport."

"What sport? What was the word?"

"Cricket."

"Cricketers, that's right. Cricketers, so that would be sport." She consults her lesson notes. "OK, so we'll just stop that activity for now."

(Adapted from Nunan, 2000: 33–35)

REFLECT

A. What three things did you notice in the vignette? Write them down in note form.

1. _____

2. _____

3. _____

B. Write down 3–5 questions you would like to ask the teacher about the lesson.

My Observations on the Vignette

There are several interesting things going on in this vignette. Here are my notes.

1. The aim of the lesson is to get the students to categorize the news items by listening for key words. She doesn't want them to try to understand every word. Even though she doesn't spell it out explicitly in this lesson, she is teaching the learners that there are different ways of listening. We don't listen to everything in the same way. Successful listeners listen in different ways according to their purpose for listening.

2. Classifying and listening for key words are strategies. The teacher thus has two complementary goals. She wants to improve the learners' listening skills and she is also working on their learning skills and strategies.

3. The one item that caused confusion was 'aboriginal cricketers.' Cricket is a game played in England and former English colonies such as Australia, South Africa, New Zealand, the West Indies and India (Although, interestingly, it never caught on in Canada in a big way.) Some people believe that you have to have been born and raised in a cricket-playing country in order to understand the game fully. Certainly, for these learners, the item was unexpected, and caused some confusion. The idea of having a cricket team composed of aboriginal players was probably also culturally unfamiliar to them. They therefore didn't have the background knowledge that would help them to make sense of what they were hearing.

4. The instructor encourages students to make inferences, that is, 'listening between the lines' and coming up with information that is not explicitly stated in the text. The issue of aboriginal cricketers is a good example of where the ability to make an inference breaks down because the students do not have the necessary background knowledge to make the inference.

Issue in Focus: Top-Down and Bottom-Up Processing

In the following quote, Richards draws a distinction between two different ways in which we process spoken language. He refers to these as bottom-up and top-down processing. Don't worry too much about words and phrases that may be unfamiliar to you such as 'lexical items' and 'phonological cues.' These will become familiar as you get further into the book. The important thing to understand is that there are two different processes going on: deciphering the 'bits' of language – individual sounds and words – on the one hand, and, on the other, using what we already know about the context of the message – the subject matter, the relationship between speakers, and so on – to make sense of what we are listening to.

> Two distinct kinds of processes are involved in listening comprehension which are sometimes referred to as "bottom-up" and "top-down" processing. Bottom-up processing refers to the use of incoming data as a source of information about the meaning of a message. From this perspective, the process of comprehension begins with the message received, which is analyzed at successive levels of organization – sounds, words, clauses and sentences – until the intended meaning is arrived at. Comprehension is thus viewed as a process of decoding. Examples of bottom-up processing in listening include the following:
>
> 1. scanning the input to identify familiar lexical items
> 2. segmenting the stream of speech into grammatical constituents
> 3. using phonological cues to identify the information focus in an utterance
> 4. using grammatical cues to organize the input into constituents – for example, in order to recognize that in "the book which I lent you"
>
> Top-down processing, on the other hand, refers to the use of background knowledge in understanding the meaning of a message. Background knowledge may take several forms. It may be previous knowledge about the topic of discourse, it may be situational or contextual knowledge, or it may be knowledge stored in long-term memory in the form of "schemata" or "scripts" – plans about the overall structure of events and the relationship between them.
>
> For example, if an adult was seated on a park bench reading aloud from a book to a group of enthralled young children, an observer would probably assume that the adult was reading a story – rather than, say, a recipe or a set of instructions on how to assemble a computer. The set of expectations for a particular kind of discourse is generated from the situation, from knowledge of a world populated by adults and children, and typical interactions between them.
>
> *(Richards, 1990: 50–51)*

When I began teaching, listening and reading were referred to as 'passive' skills, in contrast to the 'active' skills of speaking and writing. However, it is clear from the Richards extract that listening is an active process. When we listen, we do a great deal more than decode the sounds that strike our eardrums into words, phrases, and sentences. Rather, we use contextual knowledge to construct a reasonable interpretation of what a speaker has said. Contextual knowledge will include the situation, the topic of the conversation, the relationships between the speakers taking part in the conversation, as well as other factors. As Goh says:

> Listening is not just hearing. It is an active process that may begin even before the first speech signal is recognized and it may go on long after the input or spoken information has stopped. Meaning cannot be simply extracted from the sound signals, and understanding is the result of active construction occurring at all levels of text (sounds, grammar, lexis and discourse structure) and context (the topic, the participants, the communicative purpose, and the place or setting for the interaction).
>
> *(Goh, 2014: 73)*

Key Principles

1. Teach Students to Use Both Bottom-Up and Top-Down Processing

We have seen that successful listeners use both bottom-up and top-down processing. Top-down processing involves drawing on background knowledge to help make sense of what we are listening to. How do we do this? Psychologists say that we do it by drawing on schemata. Schemata are like mental movie scripts that we build up from early childhood. For example we have sets of schemata or schemas for 'going to a restaurant.' In a Western context, think how different your schema is for 'Fine dining in a French restaurant' and 'Grabbing a burger from McDonald's.' Those of you who are familiar with Japanese culture and cuisine will have very different expectations when eating in a kaiseki restaurant as opposed to eating at a tempura bar. When we learn, we constantly adjust our pre-existing schemata or add new ones. In doing so, we are living out the answer that celebrated educational psychologist David Pearson gave when he was asked to define learning. He said that learning is a process of building bridges between the known and the new, between what we already know, and what we have to learn. For me, the bridge metaphor captures the very essence of learning. Grafting new knowledge to pre-existing knowledge is also a fundamental principle in the model of learning proposed by the Swiss psychologist Jean Piaget.

2. Incorporate a Range of Text Types into Your Listening Lessons

Learners need to be exposed to a wide range of text types from monologues to dialogues, from casual conversations in which people are socializing, to interactions in which the speaker is trying to obtain goods and services. They should have the opportunity to watch all types television shows, from sitcoms to the news. Public announcements, recorded telephone messages, advertisements, and so on should also be incorporated into the listening lesson. Out of class, learners can work on their listening through the enormous range of texts available through the Internet: YouTube clips, TED talks, and also the specially modified news broadcasts from services such as the BBC and Voice of America. These have been specially recorded to be more comprehensible to second language speakers.

A much discussed concept in communicative language teaching is that of authenticity. There are two types of authenticity: text authenticity and task authenticity. Authentic listening texts are those that originally emerged in the course of some type of communication outside of the classroom – a casual conversation in a coffee shop, a news broadcast, a train announcement, and so on – and are subsequently imported into the classroom for teaching purposes. I believe there is a place in the classroom for both authentic and non-authentic texts. Both have different purposes. I have used authentic listening texts with absolute beginners. This often scares them to start with, but they become more comfortable when they realize that they don't have to understand every word. I get them to do things such as identify how many speakers there are in the conversation, or listen to several short conversations and identify which are English and which are other languages. From these experiences, my learners realize that they can benefit, and learn something; from authentic listening texts from the very beginning of the learning process. The trick is to adjust the task – what learners have to do in response to the listening – rather than the listening text itself.

3. Incorporate a Range of Pedagogical and Real-World Tasks into Your Lesson

In addition to text authenticity, there is task authenticity. Again, in deciding whether or not a task is authentic, we need to take our bearings from the world outside the classroom and ask ourselves "Is this something that people do outside the classroom?" Generally, in the real world, people don't listen to an answering machine message and complete a set of true/false questions. They listen and take a message for a third party, or make a note to themselves about where and when to meet the person leaving the message. I have already made the point that I see a place for non-authentic listening tests in the language classroom, and the same point applies to tasks. There may well be a place for true/false questions in the classroom, but there should also be tasks that enable learners to rehearse in class the sorts of things that they need to do outside the classroom.

Listening will involve production (speaking and writing tasks). The focus of a listening lesson, or a listening segment within a lesson that includes other skills, should be mainly on listening, not on speaking or writing. However, we can only evaluate whether a learner has understood a listening text by getting them to do something, that is, through production of one kind or another. This might involve answering questions, either orally or in writing, taking a telephone message, and so on. Or the response might be non-verbal: listening to a set of instructions and assembling a toy or a game, listening and drawing a picture, etc. The richer the variety of tasks the more interesting the listening lesson will be for the students, and for you, the teacher.

4. Incorporate Strategy Training into Your Teaching

Earlier in the chapter I stressed the importance of matching up our purpose for listening, with the type of aural text we're listening to, and then selecting the appropriate strategy – listening for gist, listening for key information, and so on. Purpose is paramount. As one of my favorite listening teachers, Marc Helgesen, says, ."It's not just what you're listening *to*, it's what you're listening *for*" (Helgesen, 2003: 30).

I have already spoken about the centrality of learner strategy training to my own philosophy of language teaching, and I have lots more to say during the course of this book. Mike Rost (2002: 155), another 'guru' in the language listening area, identified the following strategies of successful listeners.

- **Predicting**: effective listeners think about what they will hear.
- **Inferring**: It is useful for learners to "listen between the lines."
- **Monitoring**: Good listeners notice what they do and don't understand.
- **Clarifying**: Efficient learners ask questions (*What does _____ mean? You mean _____?*) and give feedback (*I don't understand yet*) to the speaker.
- **Responding**: Learners react to what they hear.
- **Evaluating**: They check on how well they have understood.

(For additional discussion of these and other principles, see Helgesen [2003].)

What Teachers Want to Know

The teachers posting these questions want to clarify some of the technical terms associated with listening including 'comprehensible input' and 'i+1.' They also want some practical strategies that teachers can use to make listening more comprehensible for learners.

Question: I'm still not clear about comprehensible input. I read that without access to comprehensible input second language acquisition won't happen. Can you say a bit more about comprehensible input – what exactly is it, and why is it important?

Response: Comprehensible input is language that a learner hears and can make sense of, although they may not understand every word. It's the central feature of Krashen's (1981) input hypothesis. This hypothesis suggests that in order for language learning to happen, learners must encounter language that is new and slightly beyond their current proficiency.

As instructors, we need to be aware of comprehensible input because we should strive for a balance between using language that our students are comfortable with, and introducing new words and phrases with adequate contextual cues. With too many new words, grammar will be incomprehensible. Not enough new language will limit learning opportunities for our students.

In my experience of studying Italian, it was helpful to hear my instructors use words and phrases that were not in the book but were appropriate to the subject or to the activity. For example, if we were playing a game to learn new vocabulary, the teacher might use the Italian phrase for "It's your turn." The first time I hear it, I may not remember the phrase well enough to repeat it, but I understand the basic meaning through the context in which it is used. Then, over time, after hearing the same phrase in the same context, I understand it immediately, and can even use it myself.

Question: What is i+1?

Response: Comprehensible input is a means of learning through listening to input that is challenging and slightly more difficult than one's current level of proficiency. This is known as i+1 – input plus 1. This doesn't mean that the language presented to the students is incomprehensible. Most of the language is comprehensible, but some isn't. For example, when a student comes across a conversation (or listening text in a lesson) that is slightly above their level, they can use cues given by the speaker to figure out the meaning of unknown parts. The cues can be anything from body language to pictures, or the students themselves can be encouraged to ask for a more simplified version of what is being discussed. Encouraging the students to do so will make them more comfortable using the language; thus, increasing their confidence.

This is important because if the language presented to us is too easy, then we get bored and stop listening. This doesn't only happen with second language learning, but with other subjects as well. If the content is not challenging, the learners will turn off. Likewise, when something is too difficult, learners will have a tendency to tune out. Furthermore, the students will become less motivated because they may see the language as being too difficult to learn. However, if we present language in a comprehensible way, the students' own learning can be enhanced.

Question: What can teachers do to make listening texts more comprehensible for learners?

Response: One way to make listening comprehensible is by scaffolding the learning process. As we have learned, it is important to have pre-tasks that prepare learners for the task of listening. After doing these pre-tasks, it is important to give learners a purpose for listening by requiring them to use different strategies each time they listen. Here is a procedure based on a dialogue from *Interchange* by Jack Richards to demonstrate the idea of scaffolding.

ROD: Hello.

JANA: Hi, Rod. This is Jana.

ROD: Oh, hi, Jana. What's up?

JANA: I'm going to my best friend's wedding this weekend. I'd love to take some pictures for his website. Would you mind if I borrowed your new digital camera?

ROD: Um, no. That's OK, I guess. I don't think I'll need it for anything.

JANA: Thanks a million.

ROD: Sure. Uh, have you used a digital camera before? It's sort of complicated.

JANA: Uh-huh, sure, a couple of times. Would it be OK if I picked it up on Friday night?

ROD: Yeah, I guess so.

(Richards et al., 2005: 16)

Before listening, the teacher could ask a question such as, "Listen to the conversation between Jana and Rod. What are they talking about? Don't try and understand every word – just try and get the general idea." This practices the strategy known as listening for gist, or global listening, which requires students to catch key words and to connect the words to understand the main topic.

After listening to the text the first time, the teacher could ask a question such as, "Whose wedding is this weekend?" or "When will Jana pick up the digital camera?" In answering these questions, the students are practicing a strategy called listening for specific information. Listening for specific information means that learners identify information such as a number, a name, and so on.

The third time they listen, the teacher might require learners to use a different strategy by asking them to make inferences about what they have listened to. Inferring requires students to "read between the lines" and information is not stated explicitly in the text but conclusions can be drawn based on the content provided. For the example above, the teacher could ask a question such as "How does Rod feel about Jana borrowing his digital camera?" Depending on Rod's intonation, he could sound a little irritated or concerned about Jana borrowing his camera.

TASK

Total Physical Response (TPR) is a technique for providing comprehensible input. In this technique, the teacher gives a series of instructions which students listen to and follow. If possible, in groups of 2–5, come up with an instructional sequence for providing comprehensible input through TPR.

Small Group Discussion

In the vignette presented earlier in the chapter, we saw the benefits of background knowledge, as well as the drawbacks of lack of background knowledge. In this discussion thread, the teacher and students discuss the importance of background knowledge and schemata to comprehension.

TEACHER: I'd like to begin this thread by posing two questions: Why is background knowledge important in the comprehension process? Is using background knowledge a top-down or bottom-up process?

MARI: Bottom-up processing is where you start with the smallest elements of the language and work toward the larger elements. Think, for instance, about the sounds used to make words "ship" and "sheep." Top-down processing is where you use what you already know to make sense of what you are listening to. "The president is on the ship/sheep." Using top-down processing, it makes much more sense that the president is on a ship and not on a sheep.

ROBERTO: Let's think a bit more about schema theory and background knowledge. We function on an everyday basis because we have an interior film script about how the world should behave and we use this to make sense about what is going on. We have a script for going to a restaurant. The script is different for fast food versus traditional restaurants. We always develop and modify our schema. These schemata are important in language learning, in particular listening. This sometimes can lead us into trouble when we interact with different cultures which have different schemata. And it can lead to embarrassment. We have to modify schemata according to the culture we are in.

TEACHER: There have been a number of investigations into the relationship between background knowledge and listening comprehension. These studies show that students with relevant background knowledge perform significantly better on listening tests than students who don't have the relevant background knowledge.

What other examples or experiences can you add to demonstrate that we often use background knowledge to comprehend a message?

LISA: In top-down processing, learners start from their background knowledge to understand the topic. My daughter is two years old and she usually talks by imitation. Sometimes she repeats bad words. I guess that she just listens to bad words from her friends or someone in nursery, so I don't care about it because I know that she doesn't know the meaning of those bad words. I think that's just a kind of bottom-up process. I want to ask my daughter many things and I want to communicate with her. For example, last Sunday we went to the zoo and then I asked my daughter. "Do you like tigers?" She said, "No, I'm scared of tigers." I asked again, "Why?" She replied, "The tiger bared its teeth in a snarl." Maybe she saw that in the zoo. She already knew about tigers by reading a book before that and always replied "I like tigers" to the same question. "The tiger bared its teeth in a snarl" is the possible answer after the real experience. The individual experience builds background knowledge and the background knowledge is helpful to understand something (the comprehension process). So I think background knowledge is very important in the comprehension process and is a top-down process.

TRACY: I think that using background knowledge is a top-down process. It can encourage the learners to discuss what they already know about a topic. General knowledge and life experience could help us to understand the topic. Without background knowledge, we wouldn't have a basis for making sense of the listening or reading texts that we are trying to understand.

REFLECT

Make a note of three ideas from this discussion that you would like to try out in your own teaching.

Commentary

From the discussions above, the teachers and students articulate their understanding of how background knowledge and experiences help in making sense of spoken and written messages. There are also several interesting anecdotes from their own personal experiences on the effect of background knowledge on comprehension. Students often know more than they think they do, but fail to apply that knowledge to a listening task. As teachers, it is important to remind learners of what they already know about a particular topic prior to listening to or reading a given text. If students don't have relevant knowledge, it is often possible to supply this through schema-building tasks of various kinds.

Summary

Content focus	Listening in a second language
Vignette	Listening for specific information; inferencing; authentic listening text
Issue in focus	Top-down and bottom-up processing
Key principles	1. Expose learners to different ways of processing information.
	2. Expose students to different types of listening text.
	3. Teach a variety of tasks.
	4. Consider text difficulty and authenticity.
	5. Teach listening strategies.
What teachers want to know	Comprehensible input, i+1
Small group discussion	Background knowledge, scaffolding

Further Reading

Rost, M. (2011) *Teaching and Researching Listening.* 2nd Edition. London: Pearson.

This state-of-the-art introduction to teaching and researching second language listening is thoroughly revised from the original edition which was published ten years previously. While it deals with the complexities of the linguistic, psycholinguistic, and pragmatic processes involved in the comprehension of a second language, it does so in a comprehensible and readable style. In addition to reviewing the relevant theories that have been developed, and the research that has informed the teaching of listening, the book contains many practical illustrations and examples.

References

Field, J. (2008) *Listening in the Language Classroom.* Cambridge: Cambridge University Press.

Goh, C. (2014) Second language listening comprehension: Process and pedagogy. In M. Celce-Murcia, D. Brinton, and M.A. Snow (eds.) *Teaching English as a Second or Foreign Language.* 4th Edition. Boston: National Geographic Learning.

Helgesen, M. (2003) Listening. In D. Nunan (ed.) *Practical English Language Teaching.* New York: McGraw-Hill.

Krashen, S. (1981) *Second Language Acquisition and Second Language Learning.* Oxford: Pergamon Press.

Mendelsohn, D. (1994) *Learning to Listen.* San Diego: Domine Press.

Nunan, D. (2000) *Language Teaching Methodology.* London: Pearson Education.

Richards, J.C. (1990) *The Language Teaching Matrix.* Cambridge: Cambridge University Press.

Richards, J.C. (with J. Hull and S. Proctor) (2005) *Interchange.* Students' Book 3. Cambridge: Cambridge University Press.

Rost, M. (2002) *Teaching and Researching Listening.* London: Pearson.

Rost, M. (2011) *Teaching and Researching Listening.* 2nd Edition. London: Pearson.

4

SPEAKING

Goals

At the end of this chapter you should be able to:

- distinguish between 'reproductive' speaking and 'creative' speaking
- create a range of speaking tasks including information gaps, role-plays, simulations, and speaking out-of-class assignments and projects
- define communicative competence
- identify examples of negotiation of meaning
- discuss five key principles for teaching speaking

Introduction

When we say someone knows Korean, Spanish, or any other language for that matter, we assume that they can speak the language. It would be odd if they claimed proficiency in the language on the basis of being able to read it. Of course, there are people who are fluent readers of a language but who have no facility when it comes to listening or speaking. In fact, the grammar-translation method, which dominated foreign language instruction for many years – and in some places still does – turned out learners who could read and write but who were incapable of understanding the spoken language or to speak it themselves. When I was in high school, one of my best friends was the son of Croatian immigrants. He could understand Croatian perfectly when his parents or grandparents spoke to him, but always answered them in English. When I asked him to teach me Croatian, he replied that he didn't know the language. Whether this was true, or whether there were deeper (and possibly darker) reasons for his refusal to speak

Croatian, I never knew, but I remember being disappointed that he wouldn't teach me even a phrase or two of his heritage language.

When I observe the teaching and learning of speaking, I find it useful to draw a distinction between 'reproductive' speaking and 'creative' speaking. In reproductive speaking, the learner reproduces language forms provided by the teacher or some other aural model. In the audiolingual segment of the vignette in Chapter 1, the learners were reproducing and manipulating the language models and cues provided by the teacher. In creative language use, the learners do not regurgitate the meanings of others, but create their own meanings. Both reproductive and creative language are necessary in developing speaking. Good teachers are aware of the proportion of reproductive and creative speaking work they require of their learners, and are able to match the proportions to the proficiency level and needs of their students. Often students prefer reproductive oral work because it is 'safer' as the risk of making mistakes is minimized. Again, good speaking teachers create a non-threatening environment and encourage learners to leave their comfort zone and engage in tasks that require creative language use.

Remember that, while speaking and writing are productive skills, spoken and written language are quite different. These differences manifest themselves in different ways. Spoken language has been likened to a stream of water. You will often hear references to the 'stream of speech.' One second the words hang in the air, the next second, they have vanished. How often, when we have said something, do we wish we could recall our words, revise them, and send them out again? But of course, we can't. Speech is like first draft writing. We can sometimes do a 'second draft' by saying "What I meant to say was . . ." and then cleaning up our first draft, but all too often the conversation has moved on, and we have to live with our original utterance. When we write, on the other hand, we can spend time rereading and revising what we have written until we're satisfied with it. We can even get someone else to look over it and give us feedback before 'going public.'

Vignette

The teacher, a woman in her mid-thirties, is working with a class of young teenagers in a private after-school class in Hong Kong. There are sixteen students in the class: nine girls and seven boys. She divides the class into two groups of eight, and says, "All right, group A, go and sit at the front of the class by the whiteboard. Group B, sit down in the back corner." While the students move about the classroom, she writes a list of words on the board.

When the class has reorganized itself, she directs their attention to the list of words on the board. The list includes 'sunbathing,' 'swimming,' 'deck chair,' 'volleyball.' "Do you know the meaning of these words? Check with the other members of your group. If there are any words that you don't know, look them up." When the students have finished, she hands out a set of pictures to group A, and another set to group B. "OK, so we're going to do a 'spot the difference' task today.

Your cards look almost the same, but there are some differences. Look at the cards in your groups and make sure you understand the names of all the things you see."

The pictures are almost identical. They show a beach scene. In the foreground are a boy and a girl. The boy is standing up. The girl is sitting on a folding chair. Not far away, a person is sunbathing. In the distance, two boys are playing ball. Behind the girl there is a kiosk.

"Right," says the teacher after she has given the groups several minutes to study their pictures. "Now I want one person from group A to pair up with one person from group B. I want you to sit like this – facing each other." She moves two nearby chairs so they are facing each other. "Make sure you sit facing each other, and hold up your picture so your partner can't see it. You have to describe your pictures to each other and you have to find as many differences as you can. Try to find at least five differences. There are more than five differences, but some of them might be a bit difficult, so try to find at least five."

There is some clattering in the room as the students rearrange themselves as directed. Then the room begins to buzz with voices as they set about the task. The teacher looks across at one pair and says, "Candy, hold your card up higher. Janice can see it." Then she moves about the room, monitoring the students. She pauses by one pair, and listens as they do the task.

"I have some tree, in my picture," says the boy.

"One tree?" asks the girl.

"No, some tree – three tree."

"Me too."

"So, no different."

"No different."

"And I have one man. He's lie down." When the boy says this the teacher writes something in the notebook she is holding.

"Er, one more time," says the girl.

"I say . . ."

"Yes?"

"I have one man and he's lie down."

"Mine is woman."

"So, we have one difference." They make a note in the space provided beside the picture.

The teacher moves on around the groups, occasionally making notes, offering encouragement and helping out when a student has difficulty with a word. After two minutes, she calls the class to order.

"So," she says, "How many differences did you spot?"

"Five," call out several pairs.

"Six," says a boy.

"We find eight," say another pair.

"Eight, that's great," says the teacher. "Do you know how many there are all together? Ten."

"Ten! Wah!" say several of the students.

"Now work in groups of four. You can look at each other's pictures. Now, see if the differences you spotted were the same as the other pair or different. And when you talk about the picture, use the correct form of the verb. 'Swimming,' not 'swim,' 'lying down,' not 'lie down.'" "OK Johnny," she says looking at the boy who had said 'lie down.' "Also, remember the structure we practiced the other day. 'There is/there are.' 'There's a man sunbathing in my picture.' 'There are three trees in my picture.' Off you go."

REFLECT

What 3 things did you notice in the vignette? Write them down in note form.

1. _____
2. _____
3. _____

My Observations on the Vignette

1. The 'spot the differences' task is a kind of information gap task. In tasks such as this, there is a 'gap' between the information possessed by different speakers. In the pair work segment of the task, each speaker had information that was unknown to their conversational partner. In this case, student A did not know what differences there were in student B's picture and vice versa.

2. Because of the nature of the task, it generated 'real' conversation. Notice that the girl checks that she has understood the boy correctly where she says "One tree?" A little later, she says "One more time please," meaning "Could you repeat what you said?" What she is doing is negotiating information. This negotiation of meaning in conversation is believed to be important for language acquisition. I'll describe this concept in greater detail in the Key Principles section of the chapter.

3. The language is controlled to a certain extent in that the task is designed to elicit certain grammatical structures such as 'there is/there are' and the '-ing' form of the verb. However, the learners are free to complete the task using whatever language they have at their disposal.

4. During the task itself, there is no correction of errors by the teacher because she is trying to encourage communication in which the focus is on fluency rather than grammatical accuracy. As the students complete the task, she circulates around the room and makes a note of errors that she overhears. In the

debriefing session at the end of the task, she draws these to the attention of the students.

5. The vignette exhibits the three-phase sequence of pre-task, task, and follow-up. Review the vignette and see if you can identify these three phases.

Issue in Focus: Communicative Competence

As we saw in Chapter 1, for many years, second language ability was seen in terms of linguistic competence, that is, the mastery of the sounds, the vocabulary, and the grammar of the language. It was assumed that once these elements had been mastered, a learner would have all that he or she needed to use the language to communicate. In the 1970s, however, there was a profound change in the way in which linguists and teachers conceived of the nature of language and language use (and consequently of language teaching and learning). While the ability to articulate sounds in a comprehensible manner, the possession of an adequate vocabulary, and a working knowledge of grammar were necessary, they were not sufficient for someone to communicate competently in the language. Figuring out what else the learner needed to know and be able to do in order to communicate led to the notion of communicative competence. The term was coined in the mid-1960s by the American sociolinguist Dell Hymes, and subsequently developed by Sandra Savignon, who defined communicative competence as "the ability of language learners to interact with other speakers, to make meaning, as distinct from the ability to perform on discrete-point tests of grammatical knowledge" (Savignon, 1991: 264). This ability "requires an understanding of sociocultural contexts of language use" (267).

So while communicative competence involves linguistic competence, it also involves other types of competence. According to Canadian scholars Michael Canale and Merrill Swain (1980), there are two other types of competence: sociolinguistic competence and strategic competence. In 1983, Canale added a fourth component, discourse competence. (See also, Bailey, 2003.)

In the following quote, Kathleen Bailey (2005: 3) describes the different types of competence that an individual needs to master in order to be an effective speaker:

> There are several important models of communicative competence (see, especially, Bachmann, 1990, and Canale and Swain, 1980), all of which include some form of sociolinguistic competence, or the ability to use language appropriately in various contexts. Sociolinguistic competence involves register (degrees of formality and informality), appropriate word choice, style shifting, and politeness strategies.
>
> Another important element of communicative competence is strategic competence. In terms of speaking, this is the learner's ability to use language strategies to compensate for gaps in skills and knowledge. For example, if

you don't know a word you need to express your meaning, what strategies can you use to make your point? A fourth component of communicative competence is discourse competence "how sentence elements are tied together," which includes both cohesion and coherence (Lazaraton, 2001, p. 104). Cohesion is "the grammatical and/or lexical relationships between the different parts of a sentence" (Richards, Platt, and Weber, 1985 p. 45). Cohesion includes reference, repetition, synonyms and so on. In contrast, coherence involves "how texts are constructed."

(Bailey, 2005: 3)

David Bohlke (2014) provides a complementary perspective on what it means to have competence in speaking another language. He identifies four componential skills: phonological skills, speech function, interactional skills, and extended discourse skills.

For L2 learners to communicate effectively, they must have a reasonable command of grammar and vocabulary. But this knowledge alone is insufficient. Learners need to learn a wide range of other skills. Four skill areas of speaking competence are required for effective communication (Goh, 2007).

1. *Phonological skills.* Learners need to be able to blend the phonemes of the language they are learning. In addition, they must use appropriate stress and intonation.

2. *Speech functions.* Learners need to achieve specific communicative functions in social and transactional exchanges such as agreeing with someone, asking for clarification or offering a reason.

3. *Interactional skills.* In face-to-face exchanges, learners must manage interactions by regulating turn taking, redirecting the topic, and negotiating meaning, in addition to initiating, maintaining and closing a conversation.

4. *Extended discourse skills.* Learners must often produce long stretches of uninterrupted language and they need to structure what they say so it is easy for others to follow. This requires the use of established conventions for structuring different kinds of extended spoken language such as narrative, procedural, expository, or descriptive discourse.

In addition to these four skills, the use of conversation management strategies can lead to more effective speaking. These may be strategies for enhancing one's message such as asking questions in different ways in order to be less direct, or dealing with communication breakdowns, such as rephrasing to clarify meaning. Such strategies have been identified and categorized and are now part of the syllabi of several language textbooks.

(Bohlke, 2014: 123)

Key Principles

These principles were originally articulated by Kathleen Bailey (2003) in her introduction to the teaching of speaking. In discussing principles for speaking, I have incorporated what Bailey had to say in her original formulation and have added my own commentary on the principles.

1. Be Aware of the Difference Between Second Language and Foreign Language Learning Contexts

The distinction between second language (SL) situations and foreign language (FL) situations is a long-standing one. A second language context is one where the target language (which may be English, Spanish, Chinese, Arabic, or any other language) is the main language of communication. It's also very often the official language of the country. A foreign language context is one in which the language being taught and learned is not widely used in the community. The distinction between these two contexts is important, because people learning a language in a foreign language context have limited opportunities to speak the language outside the classroom. In contrast, if you are learning a language in a country where the language is widely used, there are limitless opportunities to improve your speaking by using it for real communication in the wider community. Whether or not you choose to avail yourself of these opportunities is up to you of course.

Having said that, the distinction between second and foreign language contexts is somewhat crude or imprecise for several reasons. In the first place, economic globalization and the technological revolution have meant that numerous languages, such as English, Chinese, Spanish, and Arabic, are widely used around the world. The second reason is that the status and teaching of a language such as English will vary from country to country. The status of English, and the way it is taught, in places such as Singapore and Hong Kong, which inherited English (or had it imposed on them) because they are former colonies of Great Britain, is different from the status of English in Japan or Brazil. Again, the teaching of English in Japan is different from the teaching of English in Brazil. In addition, as I pointed out in the Introduction to this book, with the spread of English as a tool for global communication, the concept 'foreign' has become increasingly problematic.

The practical implication of this principle is that wherever you are teaching, you need to take into account the global, national, and local contexts. You also need to know how, when, and why your learners use English outside of the classroom. Talk to your students about their lives outside of class. What they tell you may surprise you.

2. Give Students Practice with Both Fluency and Accuracy

Accuracy refers to the extent to which the learners' speech is grammatically acceptable, with clear, intelligible pronunciation and appropriate choice of vocabulary.

Fluency is the extent to which the learner can speak at an acceptable speed with few false starts and hesitations. It is important to give learners opportunities to develop both aspects of their speaking. When coaching for accuracy, it is important to correct errors of pronunciation, vocabulary, and grammar, either by interrupting the speaker or by noting errors and providing feedback on them after the speaker has finished. When engaging students in fluency practice, encourage the learners to get their meaning across without worrying too much about accuracy – just as long as their speech is comprehensible and they can convey to the listener what they want to say.

When assessing a second language speaker's performance, judges sometimes use a third criterion: complexity. This is usually measured in terms of the ability of the speaker to use more complex grammatical structures such as relative clauses. You needn't concern yourself with this criterion right now. I have mentioned it because you may come across it in your reading.

3. Provide Opportunities for Students to Talk by Using Group Work or Pair Work, and Limiting Teacher Talk

This principle rests on the notion that you learn to speak by speaking. Pair and group work are the most effective way of increasing students' talking time. The only other way of giving learners an opportunity to speak in class would be for the teacher to address each student in turn. This is not an effective use of time. In a sixty-minute class, with a group of thirty students, if the entire lesson was devoted to this mode of instruction, each learner would receive less than two minutes of talking time.

Pair and group work have a number of other advantages. For example, if carefully constructed, they maximize opportunities for learners to negotiate meaning. (This concept of negotiating meaning is explained below.) They also give learners the opportunity to engage in genuine conversation, developing skills in turn-taking, speaker selection and change and so on. Speaking as a social activity is thereby promoted. Depending on your teaching context, you may find that learners don't want to talk to each other, they want to talk to the teacher. My students sometimes say, "I don't want to speak to other students because I don't want to learn their mistakes." In fact, there is no solid evidence that learners learn each other's mistakes.

In terms of teacher talk, considerable research has demonstrated that teachers take up between 50 and 80 percent of class time in speaking. While this may be great for providing learners with comprehensible input, it does little, if anything, to facilitate the speaking ability of the learner.

4. Plan Speaking Tasks that Involve Negotiation of Meaning

The negotiation of meaning refers to the interactional work that speakers do to clarify misunderstandings or to pre-empt potential misunderstandings. This process goes on all the time in normal conversation, and is such an automatic process that we usually don't even notice that we're doing it. Here are some examples.

SPEAKER A: I watched *Mad Men* last night.
SPEAKER B: Did you say *Mad Men*?
SPEAKER A: Yes.
SPEAKER A: Do you know what autodidact means?
SPEAKER B: Sorry?
SPEAKER A: Autodidact. Do you know what it means?
SPEAKER A: Tony was full of himself last night. In fact, he was as pleased as a lizard with a gold tooth, if you know what I mean.
SPEAKER B: I have no idea what you mean.

These conversational adjustments are hypothesized to be important for language acquisition because they force second language speakers to modify their speech to make it more comprehensible or understandable. Researchers have created tasks that increase the chances of misunderstanding in order to prompt learners to engage in this interactional work. They then seek to investigate the effect of this increased interactional work on language acquisition.

5. Design Classroom Activities that Involve Guidance and Practice in Both Transactional and Interactional Speaking

Michael Halliday, one of the most influential linguists of the modern era, has suggested that there are just three things that we do with spoken language. We use it to obtain goods and services, we use it to socialize, and we use it for pleasure. The first two uses, the transactional and the interactional, dominate our everyday language use and both should be built into our teaching. Halliday and others use the term 'interactional' for the second function. I prefer the term 'interpersonal,' because it highlights the fact that the second function is essentially social in nature. Also, using the term 'interactional' for the second function implies that the transactional function is not interactional. (Bear in mind that in a great many interactions transactional and social purposes are woven together, but one function will usually be the primary one.)

What Teachers Want to Know

In relation to speaking, teachers wanted to know more about techniques for activating this skill, focusing in particular on pair and group work, role-plays, simulations, and practicing speaking out of class.

Question: Why are pair and group work tasks important?

Response: Pair and group work are probably the most effective way of increasing student talking time in class. Think of a ninety-minute teacher-fronted lesson, where all eyes are on the teacher, and the interaction is from teacher to individual students. Once teacher talking time is taken into account, if there are thirty students in the class, each student will only get a few minutes of speaking time. However, if most of the lesson is devoted to pair and group work, then each student may get thirty to forty-five minutes of speaking time.

In addition, pair and group work provide learners the opportunity to engage in genuine conversation rather than rehearsing memorized dialogues or regurgitating model sentences provided by the teacher or the textbook.

Question: What are some examples of pair and group work that you have used in your teaching context?

Response: I like to use role-plays. According to Bailey (2005: 52), "A role-play is a speaking activity in which the students take the part of other people and interact using the characteristics of those people." When creating role-plays for my students, I like to think about the sorts of things that they might use the language for outside of class. So, one student might take the role of a doctor while the other is the patient; one could be the server at a restaurant while the other is the customer; one could be a taxi driver while the other is the customer who is trying to get somewhere, etc.

One role-play that I have used with my students is giving help to a tourist, for example, giving directions. Our town has many tourists, so I thought it would be helpful to do a role-play for this. In addition, we had practiced giving directions in a previous lesson. We start out by reviewing grammar and vocabulary from that lesson and I write prompts and key words on the board so that they can refer to these later if they need to. Then we brainstorm popular places in the area. I made a simplified map of our downtown area for the students to use while doing their role-plays. Each map has a different dot on it indicating the tourist's starting point. During the brainstorm, if any places are missing from the map, students can write these in. After this, I choose one "strong" student to model how to do the role-play with me. I usually take the role of the local person to take pressure off the student. The other students listen and follow along using their maps. After this, I ask them to do a role-play carrying out the same task. I give them role-play cards. For instance:

Student A – Tourist	Student B – Local person
Look at the map and decide where you want to go. Ask a local for directions.	Listen to the tourist and give directions.

Sometimes I have more specific cards, for instance, listing the place that the student wants to go to. I monitor them while they do their role-plays, making a note of their mistakes, and offering guidance if needed. I usually have them switch roles so that both students have a chance to play both roles. After they have finished their role-plays, I give them feedback and ask how they felt about the role-plays. A couple of days after this lesson, one of my students said that a foreigner had approached him for directions. He was able to help her, and he reported that this definitely boosted his confidence.

Question: What's the difference between a role-play and a simulation?

Response: In a role-play, the student is taking on the role of another person. In the example of providing directions to a visitor, the students are taking on the role of tourist and local person respectively. In a simulation, they are given an issue or problem-solving situation, and respond, not as someone else, but as themselves. For example, working in small groups, the students might be given descriptions and photos of several rental properties. Their task is to negotiate and decide which is the best place to rent. They have to decide which place they prefer on the basis of location, amenities in the neighborhood, and rental price, and then have to convince the others in the group. For one student, proximity to sporting and recreational facilities may be a priority. For another, it might be availability of public transportation. The key thing is that the learners are taking part in the task as themselves, not adopting a persona and working from role cards.

Question: Is there an advantage of simulations over role-plays?

Response: Each has advantages and disadvantages. Some students like to be themselves and put their own ideas forward. They will favor simulations. Others are reticent and like to 'hide' behind the persona provided by a role-play. Role-plays are also advantageous if the learners don't have fixed ideas about the topic at hand, or don't have the language to express their own ideas. They will also benefit from prompts and language scaffolds (for example, key vocabulary and sample language structures) that can be built into role cards. Role cards can also generate more animated discussion if conflicting opinions are built into the role cards. The problem with simulations in homogeneous or consensus-oriented classes is that the students will often all simply agree, thereby not really maximizing the potential of the task to generate language practice.

Question: What about real-life opportunities to speak outside of the classroom?

Response: The real test of a student's ability as a speaker is if they can interact with either native speakers or other users of the target language outside of the classroom. Such opportunities can be limited for those learning a language in a foreign language context, although there are many opportunities available through social networking sites on the Internet. Study abroad programs are also increasingly popular. Regardless of whether the students are studying abroad, or interacting with other speakers of the language in their own country, the out-of-class speaking opportunity needs to be structured through contact assignments. These are special speaking activities which provide a framework and objectives or outcomes for the learners. It's important to prepare learners for this type of task so they have a clear understanding of what needs to be accomplished and also to avoid embarrassing situations. In foreign language contexts, there will be tourists, exchange students, international business-people and so on who students can interact with. (For practical ideas on developing and using English out of class, see Nunan and Richards, 2015.)

TASK

Imagine that you are setting up a study abroad program for a group of students. Make a list of some of the contact assignments that you could get the students to complete. (For example: Attend a farmers' market. Find some food items such as fruit and vegetables that are unfamiliar to you. Find out about the items. What are they called? How are they grown? How are they used? Are they seasonal, or available all year round?)

How would you get the students to evaluate and report back on the experiences? (Through Facebook? An email exchange system?)

Small Group Discussion

One of the key principles discussed in the chapter concerns the importance to language acquisition of negotiation for/of meaning. In the following discussion thread, the teacher and students are discussing a technique called 'jigsaw tasks' – what they are, and why they are hypothesized to be healthy for language development.

TEACHER: What are jigsaw tasks, and why are they healthy for language development?

SU MING: This type of task is one in which an information gap exists between two or more people. In other words, one person has information and another person must use the target language in order to acquire that information.

There's one activity that I really like and I try and use it as often as possible. I would like to share some of my experiences and provide a few examples. Typically the first class is the *getting to know one another* class and for my own sake I want to create a class profile. This actually is essential as it serves several purposes. First the students get an opportunity to get acquainted with each other. Second, it enables me to know who the stronger students are and who the weaker ones are that may require more attention as the semester progresses, thus allowing me to create not just a class profile but a student profile as well. Students are required to speak to as many people in the class as possible in a given timeframe and find out as much as possible about their fellow students. Once the time is up, I divide the students into three or four groups (depending on the size of the group) so that they can create a class profile with the information they have gathered. Since it is not possible for everyone to speak to each other, students are required to ask the others in the group for more information. They then take the class profile they have created and in new groups complete the profile.

Another activity which I use a lot is one which is combined with a reading skill activity. Here the students are provided with a portion of an article, a paragraph for example. Let's assume that there are four paragraphs and four groups. Each group must extract the main points indicated in their portion. (Perhaps with secondary points which support the main point or maybe examples highlighting the main point.) Once identified, a member of each group must team up with members from each of the other groups, thus forming new groups consisting of at least one member from the original group. In their new groups, the students must take the data they have and (a) put it into a coherent order and (b) reproduce the text with just the information that they have. A member of each group must then orally summarize the text using the information at his disposal.

JEFF: Jigsaw tasks are information gap activities where two or more students have the information the others lack. I think they're a great way to integrate all the skills in a single activity as students will have to listen, write, read, and speak in order to complete the task.

Another crucial point to be mentioned is that this type of activity tends to be student-centered, allowing more time for students to produce the target language in class and it also can reduce teacher talking time. Jigsaw tasks not only make a reading exercise more challenging but also negotiation may occur among members of the groups, which is very healthy for language development.

I try to use them as often as I can as I reckon students will find this type of activity a more dynamic approach and therefore by communicating more they will benefit more as well.

TEACHER: This has been a good discussion with excellent ideas. One of the great things with jigsaw tasks is that they encourage the negotiation of meaning. The negotiation of meaning refers to when someone signals that there has been a misunderstanding or breakdown in communication in a conversation. Did any of you find anything in the literature on negotiation of meaning?

KARRIE: According to Pica, negotiation of meaning (also referred to as 'interactional adjustments') can be in the form of:

Confirmation checks: one speaker seeks confirmation of the other's previous utterance:

A: I went to the ballet last weekend.
B: *The ballet?*

Clarification request: a speaker seeks help in understanding the other's preceding utterance by saying "I don't understand"/"Repeat that, please":

> A: Did you see Brenda last night? She was stuck to James like white on rice.
> B: Sorry? *What do you mean by that?*

Comprehension checks: when a speaker checks if the listener is following the utterance or has understood the preceding utterance:

> A: You have to fold that side over like this. *Do you know what I mean?*
> B: Yeah.

Information gaps and jigsaw activities encourage the negotiation of meaning because of the way they are designed – learners have to communicate with and understand one another in order to successfully complete the activity.

Commentary

As we can see from the discussions above, jigsaw tasks are multi-directional information gaps designed to encourage learners to interact with one another in the target language in order to achieve a common goal. Some of the benefits of such tasks is that they not only encourage learners to negotiate meaning with one another to successfully complete the task, but they also increase student talk time because the learners are engaged in pair or group work.

TASK

Identify three ideas discussed by the students and teacher that you would you like to try out in your own classroom. If you are not currently teaching, what ideas would you like to know more about?

Summary

Content focus	Speaking
Vignette	Information gap/jigsaw task, 'spot the difference' task
Issue in focus	Communicative competence

Key principles	1. Be aware of the difference between second language and foreign language learning contexts. 2. Give students practice with both fluency and accuracy. 3. Provide opportunities for students to talk by using group work or pair work, and limiting teacher talk. 4. Plan speaking tasks that involve negotiation of meaning. 5. Design classroom activities that involve guidance and practice in both transactional and interactional speaking.
What teachers want to know	Pair and group work; role-plays and simulations; speaking out of class; contact assignments
Small group discussion	Information gap/jigsaw task; negotiation of meaning

Further Reading

Bailey, K.M. (2005) *Speaking*. New York: McGraw-Hill.

This book is one of the clearest and most practical introductions to speaking in a second language that is available. It contains an excellent balance between theory, research and practice in teaching and assessing speaking.

References

Bachmann, L. (1990) *Fundamentals of Language Testing*. Oxford: Oxford University Press.

Bailey, K.M. (2003) Speaking. In D. Nunan (ed.) *Practical English Language Teaching*. New York: McGraw-Hill.

Bailey, K.M. (2005) *Speaking*. New York: McGraw-Hill.

Bohlke, D. (2014) Fluency-oriented second language teaching. In M. Celce-Murcia, D. Brinton, and M.A. Snow (eds.) *Teaching English as a Second or Foreign Language*. 4th Edition. Boston: National Geographic Learning.

Canale, M. and M. Swain (1980) Theoretical bases of communicative approaches to language testing and teaching. *Applied Linguistics*, 1, 1, 1–47.

Goh, C. (2007) Teaching speaking in the language classroom. In W. Renandya and J.C. Richards (eds.) *RELC Portfolio Series*. Singapore: Regional English Language Centre.

Halliday, M.A.K. (1985) *An Introduction to Functional Grammar*. London: Arnold.

Lazaraton, A. (2001) Teaching oral skills. In M. Celce-Mercia (ed.) *Teaching English as a Second or Foreign Language*. Boston: Heinle & Heinle/Thomson Learning.

Nunan, D. and J.C. Richards (eds.) (2015) *Language Learning Beyond the Classroom*. New York: Routledge.

Richards, J., J. Platt and H. Weber (1985) *Longman Dictionary of Applied Linguistics*. London: Longman.

Savignon, S. (1991) Communicative language teaching: The state of the art. *TESOL Quarterly*, 25, 2, 261–277.

5

READING

Goals

At the end of this chapter you should be able to:

- describe the following concepts and procedures: scaffolding, integrated skills, recycling, and authentic materials
- discuss three important models of reading: bottom-up, top-down, and interactive processing
- describe three important principles for teaching reading
- discuss the characteristics and relative merits of extensive and intensive reading

Introduction

Traditionally, reading, along with listening, is characterized as a passive skill. However, reading, like listening is anything but passive, and these days we refer to reading and listening as 'receptive' rather than 'passive' skills. We know from research that both involve highly complex thinking processes. A major difference between the two is that in the case of listening, the words disappear into the air the moment they are spoken. The written word, on the other hand, exists as a permanent record. Readers can ponder over the words, and revisit them as often as they want until they are satisfied that they have reconstructed the meanings originally intended by the author.

In Chapter 3, we looked at important concepts connected with listening. These included top-down and bottom-up processing as well as schema theory. These terms are just as pertinent when it comes to reading. In reading, bottom-up processing involves decoding written symbols into sound. An example would be sounding out and blending 'c,' 'a,' 't' to come up with the word 'cat.' Top-down processing, on the other hand, involves using our pre-existing knowledge (our schemata) to make sense of what we read. Later in the chapter, we will see what Neil Anderson, an authority on second language reading, has to say about these and other important processes.

For second language learners, reading has a number of advantages. They do not need a partner in order to read, but can do it as an independent activity by themselves in their own time and space outside of the classroom. Not only does it build facility in the language, but it also fosters independent learning.

Two important functions of reading are, first of all, reading for communicative purposes, and second, reading for educational purposes. Let me explain what I mean by these two functions. Reading for communication refers to the 'real-world' purposes for reading. Think of the dozens of practical reasons why you read every day to conduct the daily business of life. Here is a partial list of the reading I did in the last twenty-four hours to obtain information I needed and to get pleasure from the printed word. I read:

- the Cathay Pacific online flight schedule for flights from Hong Kong to Los Angeles
- the dosage information on a packet of pills
- part of the chapter of a novel
- emails from my daughter who lives in the United Kingdom to find out her plans for the weekend
- the online viewing schedule of a television program to see what shows were on that night
- a couple of short stories
- a book proposal sent to me by a publisher to evaluate whether the book would be worth publishing
- the online edition of the *International Herald Tribune* for the latest news.

But we also read for educational purposes. That is, to increase our knowledge of Chinese history, for example, either because we are interested in the topic, or because we are studying it formally at school or university. Our second language students also read to consolidate their knowledge of English, and to develop the skills needed to extract information from texts written in English.

Here is an example of a reading task for educational purposes from an EFL textbook.

The task exemplifies certain aspects of reading. First, we can see that it consists of a pre-task (a) and a two-part task (b and c). It also focuses on the reading strategies of scanning and reading for key information.

a. What are the good and bad things about different kinds of transportation? Tell your partner at least one pro (good thing) and one con (bad thing) about each of these types of transportation.
bikes buses trains cars subways

b. Read the passage below. Scan the kinds of transportation the article talks about.

In North America, most students go to school by bus. The subway is also widely used in some cities. In small towns and cities, walking is still popular.

The yellow school bus is a familiar sight all over North America. It is a very convenient form of transportation because it takes students right to the entrance to the school. It also gives students a great opportunity to chat with their friends. However, the bus is slow and does not always pick up on time . . . [The article goes on to discuss the pros and cons of the subway and walking.]

c. Read the article and complete the chart.

Transportation	Pros	Cons

(Adapted from Nunan, 2005: 103)

Vignette

This class takes place with a group of adult learners in a second language classroom. The students have completed a listening comprehension exercise in which they listened to a conversation between two people who are about to go on a sightseeing excursion. They have also done a language exercise focusing on wh-questions for obtaining information about travel.

The teacher picks up a bundle of tourist brochures about a seaside resort and says, "Now, I'm going to give you some brochures about Victor Harbour, and we're going to look at what the brochure tells us. All right? It tells us where it is, how to get there, how long it takes, where you catch the train, and what you can do when you get to Victor Harbour. OK?" The students are sitting in small groups. She distributes one brochure to each group, and gives them a few minutes to skim through the brochure. Then she says, "So, when can you catch the train? When can you catch the train? What does it tell you?" She approaches one group, and indicates the place on the brochure where this information can be found. "What day is that?" she asks.

"Er, Sunday," replies one of the students.

"Sundays. Any other days?"

"Er, between June and er, August."

"Yes. Yeah, and pub . . ." The teacher's voice trails off, with a rising intonation.

The students search through the brochure. "Public holiday," says a student in another group.

The teacher smiles encouragingly. "What's a public holiday?"

"Er, Christmas," says the student.

"Exactly! Christmas, Easter. Yep. OK. That's right. And what else?"

"Wednesday and Saturday."

"Wednesdays and Saturdays and . . .?"

"School holidays," calls out a student who is sitting with a group at the back of the classroom.

The teacher nods. "Yes, OK. When it's school holidays, on Wednesday and Saturday. Now, back to the timetable. Where do you catch the train?"

There is a pause as the students scrutinize the brochure. Then one student says, "Er, Keswick."

The teacher laughs. "Kessick, yeah. A funny English word. Not Keswick, but Kessick. It's spelled Keswick, but we say Kessick. You catch it at Kessick." She then digresses for a minute to explain to the students where Keswick station is in relation to the center of the city. She then continues. "Remember when we were listening to the tape? One of the people said 'I'll go to the tourist bureau.' You know 'tourist bureau'? Special office. And get these." She waves a brochure. "What do the brochures tell you? What do brochures tell you? What do brochures tell you?" She pauses and smiles encouragingly, waiting for a response.

Finally, one of the students says, "How can we catch the train, and . . ."

"That's right," interjects the teacher.

". . . how much it, er, the ticket cost."

"Good. It tells you about the place, it tells you how to get there, where to catch the train, how long it takes, how much it costs. And this one also tells you about eats and drinks – eats and drinks – OK? What you can get on the train. Now, I would like you to work in little groups, just where you are. I'll give you another brochure. Have a look at something you'd like to do and see what information you can find out. Where is it? How do you get there? How much it costs. What time it leaves." She distributes a new brochure to the groups. "And I'll come round and help you."

The students begin looking at the brochures in their groups, and the teacher moves around the room asking the students questions and encouraging them.

(Adapted from Nunan, 2000: 78–80)

REFLECT

What 3 things did you notice in the vignette? Write them down in note form.

1. _____
2. _____
3. _____

My Observations on the Vignette

1. The teacher builds on a previous listening lesson about the same topic. This integrated skills approach mirrors the way language is used in everyday life. There are times when we read, to the exclusion of listening, speaking, and writing. There are other times when we listen to the exclusion of the other skills. More often, however, we use at least one other skill. We might listen to a recorded message and record key points from the message in writing. We might read an interesting news item and tell a friend or partner about it.

2. Recycling topics and content from a prior listening lesson enables the learners to use what they already know to learn something new. This is a good example of a top-down approach to reading when the learners use prior knowledge to make sense of what they are reading. (The next section discusses in greater detail exactly what we mean by top-down reading.)

3. The students are introduced to a particular type of written genre: the tourist brochure. The teacher directs their attention to an important purpose of tourist brochures, which is to provide factual information. Through her questioning technique, she gets them to practice a specific reading strategy – scanning for specific information.

4. Linguistically, the lesson reinforces a prior grammar lesson that focused on wh- questions. The learners get to practice these questions in an authentic context, and hopefully they will appreciate this real-world purpose for using this grammatical form.

Issue in Focus: Models of Reading

Three models have been proposed for the reading process. These are bottom-up reading, top-down reading, and interactive reading. The notions of bottom-up and top-down processing should be familiar to you from Chapter 3, where I discussed them in relation to listening. In this chapter, you will see how we can also use the concepts to help us understand the reading process.

In reading texts written in alphabetic languages such as English, bottom-up reading begins by matching individual letters of the alphabet with their corresponding sound and then blending these together to form words. As I mentioned earlier in the chapter, in reading the word *cat*, we mentally sound out the letter 'c,' 'a,' 't,' then blend these together to form the word 'cat.' Words are combined to form phrases, clauses, and sentences, and then these are combined to form longer stretches of text such as paragraphs.

A very popular and prominent approach to the teaching of reading, called phonics, was based on the bottom-up model. This approach has been around for many years, and is probably the most widely used method of teaching reading in English still in existence today. In the approach, learners are taught to decode letters from their written to their aural form and then to blend these together to form words along the lines described in the previous paragraph.

This process of decoding individual letters into their matching sounds as a way of reading may seem obvious. However, there are a number of problems with the bottom-up model and with the phonics approach to teaching reading. In the first place, there are many more sounds in a language like English than there are letters of the alphabet. In the case of English, there are almost twice as many sounds as there are letters. Many letters therefore have to do double duty and represent more than one sound. Take the letter 'c,' for example. It can represent a hard 'k' sound, as in 'cat,' or a soft 's' sound as in 'ceiling.' So, when someone who is learning to read English encounters a word containing the letter 'c,' how do they decide whether the letter represents a 'k' sound or an 's' sound? How do they know whether the word spelled C-A-T is sounded 'kat' or 'sat'? Does the word refer to a small, furry pet or the act of sitting down? I'll address this problem in a moment.

Another problem with the bottom-up theory of reading is that it just takes so long to transform symbols into sounds. If we were required to match every letter we come across with their corresponding sounds, we would most likely forget the beginning of a sentence before we got to the end. Just imagine how long it would take to read a lengthy novel of several hundred pages, or the Harry Potter saga with its thousands of pages.

Critics of bottom-up reading came up with their own model – top-down reading. According to this model, the reader begins with an hypothesis, or set of hypotheses, about the meaning of a text that they are reading. Anderson (2008: 6) suggests that top-down reading:

> begins with the idea that comprehension resides in the reader. The reader uses background knowledge, makes predictions, and searches the text to confirm or reject the predictions that are made. Grabe and Stoller (2002) point out that in a top-down model of reading, comprehension is directed by the reader's goals and expectations. A reading passage can thus be understood even if not all of the individual words are understood. Within a top-down approach to reading, the teacher focuses on meaning-generating

activities rather than on mastery of the bottom-up skills of letter, sound and word recognition.

The top-down model, in turn, has its own critics. Principal among these is the argument that if the reader is constantly having to generate and test hypotheses, reading takes even longer than decoding. Another problem is that if the reader does not have the relevant background knowledge, then he or she has nothing to draw on to develop and test hypotheses.

These days, the approach that is generally accepted as the most adequate explanation of the reading process is an interactive one. This approach:

> combines elements of both bottom-up and top-down approaches. The best readers in any language are those who combine elements of both. For example, most readers begin reading by using top-down reading strategies until there is a problem and then they shift to bottom-up strategies. Have you ever read something quickly and suddenly come to several new words? You are required to slow down your reading to decode the new words. When you do this, you are using bottom-up strategies to understand the words.
>
> *(Anderson, 2008: 5–7)*

Key Principles

In his introductory article on second language reading, Neil Anderson (2003) sets out eight principles for teaching reading. In this section, I have selected three of these principles for comment.

1. Build a Strong Vocabulary Base

An extensive vocabulary is important for all aspects of language use, none more so than reading. The more limited the learner's vocabulary, the less will be his or her ability to communicate. Interestingly, a basic tenet of audiolingualism, one of the most popular of all teaching methods, was that vocabulary teaching should be strictly limited. The focus of the method was on the teaching of grammatical patterns using techniques that I described in Chapter 1. With beginners, it was thought that teaching extensive vocabulary at the same time as teaching the grammar patterns would place too much load on the learner's memory. With the development of communicative language teaching, all that changed, because, as I have said, without the words to express our ideas, communication is impossible. (I will come back to this point in Chapter 8, when I look at vocabulary in detail.)

Theory and research have shown that extensive reading is one of the most effective ways of developing a rich vocabulary. In deciding which words to teach and how to teach them, Anderson recommends that we ask ourselves the following questions, which he has taken from Nation (1990: 4). (See also, Nation, 1997, 2004.)

1.   What vocabulary do my learners need to know?
2.   How will they learn this vocabulary?
3.   How can I best test to see what they need to know and what they now know?

2. Teach for Comprehension

In my view, too much time in the reading classroom is spent on testing rather than teaching. Learners are given a passage to read, and this is followed by a set of comprehension questions designed to see how much information they have extracted from the text. In this read-then-test approach, the focus is on the end result of reading, rather than on the reading process itself. It is important for readers to be thinking about what they're doing as they read, a process that Anderson refers to as comprehension monitoring. A useful technique for doing this is called 'questioning the author' (Beck *et al.*, 1997). As the term suggests, learners are taught to ask questions as they read a text. The questions might include: *What is the author trying to tell me here? How does this connect with what he wrote in the previous paragraph? What's the author's most important point here?*

3. Encourage Readers to Transform Strategies into Skills

Strategies are 'the mental and communicative processes that learners deploy to learn a second language. For example, memorizing, inductive learning, deductive learning' (Nunan, 1999: 310). Strategies are very important, as they are tools that allow the learner to begin to take control of their own learning. I've already had something to say on this subject, and will have quite a bit more to say in the course of this book. In fact, the penultimate chapter is devoted entirely to the subject of strategies.

In the vignette you studied earlier in this chapter, the teacher focused on the strategy of scanning for specific information. This is a key strategy in many kinds of reading, and one that good readers use very effectively.

One or more strategies will be inherent in any reading task. When the teacher instructs the learners to look quickly through a text to find key words, without expecting them to understand everything, she is getting them to use the strategy of scanning. Skills, on the other hand, reside within the language user. When a learner has practiced a particular strategy to the point where he or she can apply it automatically, without consciously having to do so, we can say they have acquired the strategy as a skill.

What Teachers Want to Know

In this section, questions about extensive reading, intensive reading, and graphic organizers are answered.

Question: We've read about the benefits of extensive reading, but how can we encourage our students to become extensive readers?

Response: As with many aspects of language learning, modeling and giving learners concrete examples are great ways to encourage extensive reading. I talk to my learners about my own experience as a language learner, and that really helps to give credibility to what I'm saying because I'm not just speaking as a teacher but also as a language learner. So, for example, when I was learning Spanish, I used to do lots of reading outside the classroom. I've always enjoyed reading in English, and so I wanted to be able to read fluently in Spanish as well. I've always advocated extensive reading to my own students, so I thought that I should give it a go myself. Unfortunately, my Spanish reading class was pretty traditional. The teacher would make us read short passages and then give us comprehension questions on the passages to test how much we had learned. This was useful, but the problem was that the passages were often boring to me. Another problem was that many of the passages we had to read were way too hard. So I started my own extensive reading program outside the classroom. In the beginning, when my level was low, the problem of difficulty was a major one – just as it was inside the classroom. It was impossible for me to understand books written in Spanish for native speakers, so I started with books for young teens. I also used a technique that I learned from Neil Anderson for increasing speed and fluency. I would read part of a text as fast as I could for three minutes, and mark the spot I had gotten to. Then I'd reread the passage a second time. I understood a lot more the second time, and got further down the passage. I'd count the number of words I'd read on both readings, and record them in a chart. I found this really motivating, and my reading fluency really began to increase.

When you encourage your learners to read extensively outside the classroom, make sure that you emphasize the fact that they should be reading for meaning. They should be discouraged for looking up every unknown word in their dictionary. This will slow up the reading process and end up turning the readers off. So tell them to ignore unknown words. Remember, extensive reading involves reading a lot with the goal of overall understanding, not 100 percent comprehension. Learners should be working with texts that are easy for them and their aim should be to gain pleasure from the process.

Question: Can you tell us a bit more about the purposes and benefits of intensive reading?

Response: Intensive reading involves the detailed reading of shorter texts than extensive reading. The goal is 100 percent comprehension as well as an explicit focus on language features such as grammar items and unknown vocabulary. In intensive reading, the use of a dictionary is encouraged. We have already discussed the distinction between fluency and accuracy in relation to speaking, and the same goes for reading. Extensive reading is a fluency-oriented activity, while intensive reading is accuracy-oriented.

Question: What is a graphic organizer, and how can it help in the reading process?

Response: Graphic organizers, which go by a number of other names including mind maps, concept maps, and advance organizers, are visual representations of the content or concepts in a written text. Most also show the relationships between the concepts. In other words, they present the content of the text as a visual rather than as a continuous stream of written words. There are many ways in which they can be used. At the pre-task stage of a lesson, for example, you could give your students a graphic organizer, and ask them to study it and discuss the ideas contained in it. The students could then read a text on which the graphic organizer is based. At the task stage of the lesson, learners could be required to create their own graphic organizer by, for example, reading a text and transforming the content into a table, chart, diagram, or concept map. This task can be made easier for weaker students if you give them a partially completed graphic organizer.

TASK

Complete this graphic organizer comparing and contrasting extensive and intensive reading

EXTENSIVE READING		INTENSIVE READING
	Type of processing that is encouraged	
	Purpose	
	Level of comprehension required	
	Degree of difficulty	
	Amount of reading	
	What learners do with unknown words	
	Reading text chosen by	

Small Group Discussion

In this thread, a small group of TESOL teachers are discussing the interactive approach to the reading process based on several overview articles that they have been reading.

JANA: I understand bottom-up processing and top-down processing, but I'm still a bit confused about the interactive approach. I'm also not sure about Anderson's claim that it's the best description of what happens when we read.

ISOBEL: My understanding is that an interactive approach brings together both bottom-up and top-down reading processes. In the bottom-up approach, the reader starts with the smallest bits of the language, the individual letters – graphemes I think they were called in one of the readings – and use these to understand words, and then from words to sentences. In the top-down approach, readers start with the overall context, the 'big picture,' and use their own background knowledge of the content, situation, or topic to make predictions about the content of a text. They then read the text to confirm their predictions or disconfirm their predictions. In the interactive approach, they use both processes. They attack the reading process from both ends, as it were. So they might begin with a top-down approach, and when they come across a word they don't understand, they might try and figure out the meaning according to the sentence context in which the word occurs. For example, they might identify the part of speech and use that to help them figure out the meaning. This combination is the best description of what happens when we read because we do decode unfamiliar words and we do predict what is next according to our knowledge of the word.

JOSE: According to my reading of Anderson, the interactive approach to reading combines elements of both top-down and bottom-up models. He says top-down models assume that comprehension resides in the reader. The reader's background knowledge enables the reader to make predictions about what is to come next. The reader may not know all the words but is able to understand the overall intention of the writer. On the other hand, in a bottom-up model, students start with the fundamentals like letter recognition building up to words, and arriving at whole texts in order to achieve comprehension. By combining the elements of both models a student of a second language can effectively integrate these to achieve comprehension.

I think this is the best description because there is a natural tendency for students who read something to make a connection with what they already know about a subject. If we are reading for pleasure, for example a novel, we have a tendency to read similar genres and therefore know what to expect in the stories. Love stories or fantasy stories come to mind. Similarly when it comes to work or study, the texts we read are familiar because we see these on a daily basis. We are able to get the general idea and make predictions. However, crucial details may be missed since they would need to decode unfamiliar language or vocabulary. Thus a bottom-up approach would be necessary in order to gain full comprehension of the text that is being read. Thus, the interactive approach is the best description because as one gains more proficiency in the language, the integration of the top-down and bottom-up approach becomes more natural.

DAN: This reminds me of Piaget's theory of learning.

JANA: Can you tell us about this theory, Dan? I'm not familiar with it.

DAN: Well, he argues that knowledge grows when new knowledge gets attached to existing knowledge. When the new knowledge gets incorporated into existing knowledge, Piaget calls it assimilation. When the new knowledge changes or transforms the existing knowledge it's called accommodation. I think that both of these processes are at work when we read interactively.

ISOBEL: But, I don't quite get it. What's this got to do with language?

DAN: It has to do with language and content, and the interaction between what we already know and what we have to learn. It might be pushing the concept a bit, but I still think it's a valid way of looking at how we make sense of what we read, and how we learn from reading.

SANDRA: There are problems with both bottom-up and top-down processing. By itself, bottom-up processing can't account for how we're able to read, because it neglects the reader's contribution to the process of constructing meaning, and sees reading as a mechanical process of decoding rather than as a process of interacting intelligently with the text. On the other hand, top-down processing overemphasizes prediction at the expense of knowledge of language. It seems to me that the interactive approach is a compromise between the two.

DAN: Has anyone had any experience of actually trying out the interactive approach in the classroom?

SANDRA: I have. Well, I *think* I have. My upper-intermediate students are required to read one book a semester, so for the reading part of their course, I plan an entire semester's worth of work. Before they actually read the book, I give them stuff to read about the author as well as information to build up their background knowledge of the subject of the book. And I don't just get them to read, I do things like create little quizzes that they can do in small groups. Then, when they start reading the novel or whatever the book is, I work on aspects of language, vocabulary building, exploring aspects of grammar, such as why, in a narrative, the author switches between past and present tenses. Sometimes, I get them to rewrite a few paragraphs, changing the tenses from the original or switching from third person to first person – that sort of thing. They find it fun, it develops their feeling for language, and they can begin to appreciate the difference that making these changes makes to meaning. At the same time, in class, we have what we call reading circles where students in small groups share their opinions and ideas about what they're reading.

DAN: Do your students actually do any reading of the text in class?

SANDRA: Very little. Most of their reading is done outside of the classroom. Class time is for structured learning opportunities.

Commentary

From the discussions above, we see the necessity for learners to take an interactive approach to reading, combining their background knowledge and experiences with their knowledge of the language or parts of the language. As teachers, we should provide learners with opportunities for top-down, bottom-up, and interactive processing through intensive reading and extensive reading. We can also facilitate the development of reading skills by the types of pre-tasks and tasks that we create for learners to undertake in connection to these readings. At first, some students struggle with the idea of reading an entire book – many of them haven't actually done this. But as the semester continues, they really get into it, and they say to me how much they're enjoying it. The secret is to get them involved, and encouraging them to make their own contributions to the learning process.

TASK

Select a short text (it might be fiction or non-fiction) and, drawing on the principles and ideas in the above discussion, construct a lesson for teaching the text.

Summary

Content focus	Reading in a second language
Vignette	Scaffolding, integrated skills, recycling, authentic materials, reading for specific information
Issue in focus	Models of reading: bottom-up, top-down, and interactive reading
Key principles	1. Build a strong vocabulary base.
	2. Teach for comprehension – read-then-test, comprehension monitoring; questioning the author.
	3. Encourage readers to transform skills into strategies.
What teachers want to know	Extensive reading, intensive reading, graphic organizers
Small group discussion	Interactive processing

Further Reading

Anderson, N. (2008) *Reading*. New York: McGraw-Hill.

This is a clear, concise, and insightful introduction to the teaching of reading as a second and foreign language. It looks are the nature of the reading process before turning to specific techniques for teaching readers at different levels of proficiency: beginners, intermediate, and advanced learners. The final chapter sets out key issues for teachers to consider such as the teaching of strategies, the importance of silent, oral, and extensive reading, and the professional development of the reading teacher.

References

Anderson, N. (2003) Reading. In D. Nunan (ed.) *Practical English Language Teaching*. New York: McGraw-Hill.

Anderson, N. (2008) *Reading*. New York: McGraw-Hill.

Beck, I., M. McKeown, R. Hamilton, and L. Kucan (1997) *Questioning the Author: An Approach for Enhancing Student Engagement with Text*. Newark: International Reading Association.

Grabe W. and F. Stoller (2002) *Teaching and Researching Reading*. New York: Pearson Education.

Nation, I.S.P. (1990) *Teaching and Learning Vocabulary*. New York: Newbury House.

Nation, I.S.P. (1997) The language learning benefits of extensive reading. *The Language Teacher*, 21, 5, 3–16.

Nation, I.S.P. (2004) Vocabulary learning and intensive reading. *EA Journal*, 21, 2, 20–29.

Nunan, D. (1999) *Second Language Teaching and Learning*. Boston: Heinle/Cengage.

Nunan, D. (2000) *Language Teaching Methodology: A Textbook for Teachers*. London: Pearson Education.

Nunan, D. (2005) *Go For It*. 2nd Edition. Student Book 2. Boston: Heinle/Cengage.

6

WRITING

Goals

At the end of this chapter you should be able to:

- provide an account of the nature of the writing process
- discuss the advantages and disadvantages of the product and process approaches to writing
- describe four important principles for teaching writing
- discuss the relationship between classroom and real-world writing tasks
- discuss the concept of contrastive rhetoric and its implications for the writing classroom

Introduction

Unless you're obsessed with the art and the craft of writing, as I have been from the time that I could first hold a pencil, you probably find writing to be a bit of a chore when you have to do it. In this chapter, I try and convey some of my own enthusiasm for the writing process. The overall aims of the chapter are to provide insights into the nature of the writing process, along with practical approaches and methods for teaching writing to second language learners. Like reading, writing is not only a tool for communication but also an instrument for intellectual growth and development.

Earlier in the book, I said that listening and reading were often grouped together because they are receptive skills, and that speaking and writing were placed together because they are productive skills. However, another way of grouping the four skills is in terms of mode of communication. Here the distinction is between visual and aural. These different ways of characterizing the four skills can be represented schematically as follows.

	Productive	Receptive
Visual	Writing	Reading
Aural	Speaking	Listening

Maggie Sokolik (2003), a leading thinker and researcher in the field of second language writing, suggests that writing can be defined in terms of three key contrasts. First, she says, writing is both a physical as well as a mental act. On the surface, writing is a manual process of committing symbols (letters of the alphabet, etc.) to paper or a computer screen by manipulating a pencil, pen, or keys on a keyboard. On the other hand, writing is a mental process of generating ideas and thinking about how to present them effectively in the form of a written text. Second, there are two purposes: to express and impress. "Writers," she says, "typically serve two masters: themselves, and their own desires to express an idea or feeling, and readers, also called the audience, who need to have ideas expressed in certain ways" (Sokolik, 2003: 88). The third contrast that Sokolik draws is between process and product. Process refers to the steps that a writer goes through in order to create a piece of written work. The product is the end result: the essay, recipe, report on a science experiment, and so on, which you can hold in your hand or see on a computer screen. I have more to say about the process/product distinction, and the implications the distinction holds for teaching, in the 'issues' section that follows the vignette.

Before turning to the vignette, however, I want you to think about why we write. Why is it that writing systems evolved in different societies thousands of years ago? (And, bear in mind that some languages and cultures never evolved writing systems.)

Here are some of the reasons why writing systems may have evolved:

- To provide a more-or-less permanent record of some event. Records come in many shapes and forms: from records of the weather for a particular city over the course of a year, to a personal diary kept by someone over the course of their life.
- To communicate with someone else who is distant in time and space by means of letters, postcards, or emails.
- To entertain or instruct through creative literature such as stories, novels, and poems.
- To present complex arguments that would be beyond the spoken word in the form of essays, journal articles, and so on.
- To remind ourselves of things we need to do: shopping lists, notes in a weekly planner.

In the introduction to Chapter 5, I drew a distinction between reading for 'real-world' purposes, and reading for 'educational' purposes – that is, reading for learning. The same can be said for writing. Think about the reasons why *you* write. To stimulate your thinking, here are some of the texts I produced for real-world purposes in the last twenty-four hours.

I wrote:

- part of the second draft of the chapter that you are reading now
- a recipe for mushroom risotto that a friend requested
- an email to my daughter who lives in another country
- a report on a doctoral thesis that I am examining
- a shopping list
- a PowerPoint presentation to accompany a talk that I am giving next week
- the first draft of a column that I regularly contribute to the *Tokyo Journal*.

Although I have drawn a distinction between writing for real-world purposes and writing for learning, there should be a link between the two purposes. In the following sample task, the learners are practicing writing an invitation, and also the question form with modal verbs 'Would you like to . . .?' 'Could you . . .?' However, these are skills that they can transfer to the real world. The task is presented in two parts: a pre-task, and the task proper.

WRITING

a.   Imagine you are having a party. Decide on the details below.

What kind of party?

Day/Date

Time

Place

Directions

How many people?

b.   Write an email invitation to your party.

MESSAGE

Accept Reply Forward Delete Print Move
Dear,

(Source: Adapted from Nunan, 2005: 110)

Vignette

The scene for this vignette is a sixth-grade classroom of intermediate English language learners in a school with a high proportion of immigrant students. The teacher is working on a unit on neighborhoods. In a previous lesson, the students listened to three students discussing the topic of 'My ideal neighborhood,' in which they discussed the kind of facilities and services that they would like in their ideal neighborhood. This was followed by a parallel reading text on the same topic which was intended as a vocabulary enrichment task. The teacher then placed large pictures of three neighborhoods on the board, and encouraged students to talk about which neighborhood they would prefer and why. In this part of the lesson, she focused the students on the grammatical structure 'would like/wouldn't like' as well as the interrogative (question) 'Would you like . . .?' The lesson then concluded with the teacher asking the students to write a 200-word piece about their ideal neighborhood using the reading passage as a model. They had the weekend to do this and were instructed to bring the piece to class on the following Monday. She handed out a set of guidelines to help them complete the task. This vignette takes place on the following Monday morning.

The teacher chats with the students about their weekend.

"So, what did you do on the weekend . . .? Ling?"

"Homework," says Ling.

The rest of the class laughs. "Homework. Homework," several of the other students echo.

"Great!" says the teacher. "I'm so glad that you all got your homework done. Take it out now, please."

While the students take out their homework, she circulates and looks at several of the pieces to check that the students have carried out the task as instructed, including adhering to the word length. Most of the pieces are handwritten, although several have been completed on a word processor.

"Now," she says, "I want you to get into pairs, and we're going to . . . What are we going to do Alicia?"

"Peer review."

"Peer review. And you all know how to do this. So get into your pairs with your peer review partner, and exchange pieces. I'll come around and give you a peer review sheet."

PEER REVIEW COMMENT SHEET

Written by:

Date:

Read your partner's paper. Answer these questions.

1. Is the introduction clear? Explain your answer.
2. Is the author's ideal neighborhood in the city, the suburbs, or the country?
3. Does he or she give a reason. Restate it here.
4. Does the author identify three facilities or services they would like in their ideal neighborhood?

5. Does he/she support these with reasons?
6. Does the author write about anything they would not like in their ideal neighborhood?
7. Is there a conclusion, restating and summarizing the piece?
8. Are there any grammar mistakes? Circle these.

The students work individually for fifteen minutes, reading their partner's piece and making notes on their comment sheet. The teacher walks around the room ensuring that all students are on task. Then she claps her hands and calls the class to attention.

"All right," she says. "Now it's time to conference with your partner. Ready? Alexis, ready?"

"Ready," replies a boy sitting at the back of the room.

"Good. Off you go, then."

The students spend ten minutes giving each other feedback before the teacher once again calls them to attention.

"So," she says, "I want a brief report from each of you. I want you to tell us what you learned from the peer review, what changes you're going to make in your final draft. Sunil, can you go first, please?"

"My introduction," he says, and then hesitates.

"Yes, what about your introduction."

"Don't have it . . ." his voice trails off. The rest of the class laughs. Sunil grins.

"So you need to add an introduction," says the teacher. "Anything else? What about grammar?"

"Grammar OK, Miss."

The teacher looks surprised. "Who was your partner? Alexis, was it?"

Sunil nods and says, "The grammar. He don't say nothing."

"Well, maybe you can come and conference with me during the morning break."

The teacher continues around the class, getting an oral report from each student about what they need to do to improve their piece in light of the peer review session. She then says, "All right. That was very, very useful. I want you to use the feedback you got from your partner to do a final draft, OK. I'll give you until Friday. You can give me your final draft on Friday."

REFLECT

What 3 things did you notice in the vignette? Write them down in note form.

1. _____
2. _____
3. _____

My Observations on the Vignette

1. The first thing to note is how carefully the teacher scaffolds the learning. Prior to the writing class, the learners have taken part in a listening and a reading lesson as well as receiving instruction on a key grammar point. These provide the learners with key content, grammar, and vocabulary as well as a model of the kind of text that they are expected to produce. When it comes to producing their own text, the learners have been well-prepared to complete the task.

2. Another notable feature is that class time is used for learning, not writing. The learners do their writing out of class, which enables the teacher to devote lesson time to productive learning tasks. For me, this is ideal, although it is not always feasible, as I indicated in the introduction. Sometimes you will find yourself in situations where the learners, through circumstance or choice, are unable to, or do not want to, do writing independently out of class.

3. The bulk of the lesson is devoted to collaborative peer teaching and learning, with the students exchanging their writing pieces and completing a guided evaluation. Again, there may be contexts in which this is neither feasible nor desirable. A potential stumbling block is the attitude many learners have that they cannot learn from each other, that it is only the all-knowing teacher who can provide them with productive feedback. In the right circumstances, however, it can be a highly productive activity as it engenders a reflective critical and self-critical attitude on the part of the learners. This type of activity is typical of the process approach to teaching writing which I will talk about in the next section.

4. The teacher personalizes the learning by creating a task that allows the learners to describe and justify their own ideas and preferences in relation to the topic of 'my ideal neighborhood.' This is a great illustration of the notion that learning is a process of building bridges between what the learners already know, and what you want them to learn. They begin with, but then go beyond, what they already know.

5. A final point to note is that the teacher reveals to the learners, through the inductive nature of the task, the generic structure of this kind of text in which the writer is required to present a personal point of view and then support it with an appropriate argument.

Issue in Focus: The Process Versus Product Debate

Probably one of the more contentious issues in the teaching of writing to second language speakers has been the controversy over product versus process approaches to instruction. As the name suggests, product-oriented approaches focus on the final product, that is, the final text that the writer will produce. Process-oriented approaches, on the other hand, focus on the procedures involved in arriving at the final product – the thinking, planning, drafting, and revising that the writer engages in to arrive at an acceptable text.

In a product-oriented classroom, learners spend much of their time studying and then imitating model texts provided by the teacher or the textbook. Teachers concentrate on ensuring grammatical accuracy at the sentence level, the sentence being seen as the basic building block of the text. Proponents of process approaches argue that the product approach is mechanical and cripples the creativity of the writer.

In the process-oriented classroom, learners spend a great deal of time engaged in activities other than writing. In their book on process writing, White and Arndt (1991) suggest a thirteen-step process as writers progress from initial ideas to the production of a final text.

1. Learners engage in discussion as a whole class, and in small groups and pairs.
2. They brainstorm, making notes and asking questions.
3. They then do fast-writing, selecting ideas and establishing a viewpoint without worrying about such things as errors of punctuation, spelling, or grammar.
4. Based on the fast-writing phase, they produce a rough draft.
5. They then carry out a preliminary evaluation of what they have written.
6. They then focus on the arrangement of information and the structure of the text.
7. A first draft is then produced.
8. Groups and peers evaluate and respond to other students' drafts.
9. Learners take part in a conference, discussing their drafts and deciding on what changes to make as they produce a second draft.
10. The second draft is written.
11. The writer self-evaluates the second draft, focusing on accuracy through proofreading and editing.
12. A finished draft is produced.
13. Peer readers provide a final response to the draft.

Think of the vignette presented above. This is taken from a process-oriented classroom. What stage are the learners in this classroom working through?

As you can see from the thirteen-step procedure, the process approach requires writers to produce multiple drafts, getting feedback on successive drafts as they get closer to a desired final product. If writing by hand rather than on a computer, this can be extremely time-consuming and tedious, and it has been suggested that the process approach really only became feasible with the advent of word processors.

The process approach has been subjected to numerous criticisms. One of these is that, while the approach fosters creativity and creative writing, it does not foster factual writing. Not surprisingly, left to select their own subjects, young writers tend to choose personal narratives. In fact, personal writing, and rooting the writing in personal experience, are encouraged. According to linguists such as

Jim Martin, left to themselves young writers will not develop mastery of the factual genres that are necessary to succeed in high school. Factual writing fosters critical thinking skills. Another critic, Rodrigues, makes a similar point, arguing that the unfettered writing that is fundamental to the process approach does not provide young writers with sufficient support.

> Students need structure, they need models to practice, they need to improve even mechanical skills, and they still need time to think through their ideas, to revise them, and to write for real purposes and real audiences.
>
> *(Rodrigues, 1985: 26–27)*

My own view is that the product and process approaches are not in opposition but are complementary. There is no reason why both approaches can't be integrated in the writing class, in the same way as accuracy- and fluency-oriented activities can be integrated in the speaking class, and both extensive and intensive reading can be incorporated in the reading class.

Key Principles

I have taken these principles from Maggie Sokolik (2003) and provided my own interpretations of them. If you are interested, you might like to look at what Sokolik has to say about the principles.

1. Understand Your Students' Reasons for Writing

As we saw in Chapter 2, making reference to the student when deciding what to teach, how to teach, and how to assess is fundamental to a learner-centered approach to instruction. A learner-centered curriculum will contain similar elements as a traditional curriculum. However, the key difference is that in a learner-centered curriculum the learners and their needs take center stage (Nunan, 2013). According to Sokolik, in the writing classroom, mismatches between the goals of the teacher and those of his or her learners is the greatest source of dissatisfaction on the part of learners. Awareness of how a writing course fits in to the rest of the curriculum is fundamental. Are the students required to do technical writing such as report writing, or is the writing component largely intended to support oral language development or the mastery of grammar?

2. Provide Many Opportunities for Your Students to Write

This principle reflects the philosophy of learning by doing. Just as we can improve our speaking by having lots of speaking practice, so we improve our writing by having lots of writing practice. But the actual writing should be supported by reflecting on the process and by getting feedback on the ensuing product.

The other relevant point here is the need for variety. In a specific purpose writing course, the range of written genres, or text types, will be restricted to and reflect the overall nature of the course. For example, in a business-writing course, the focus will be on genres such as report writing. In a general English course, there will be greater scope for extending the range and variety of writing types. (Sokolik lists short responses to reading texts, journal entries, letter writing, summarizing, poetry, or "any type of writing you find useful in your class should be practiced in class" [2003: 93].)

I like the variety of writing types that Sokolik lists. However, in my own teaching I have a dilemma. Ideally, I would like class time to be oriented to the process approach: peer discussion of writing drafts, and conferencing with the teacher rather than the production of texts. Ideally, students should produce their drafts in their own time outside of the classroom, rather than in the class. However, with the class I currently teach, not all students do the work outside of class. It is there-fore necessary for me to provide in-class opportunities for writing.

3. Make Feedback Helpful and Meaningful

This may seem a truism. However, all too often the brief written comments on a piece of writing are opaque. 'Unclear,' 'Not up to your usual standard,' 'Watch your grammar' give little direction to the students about what they should do in order to improve their writing. Feedback can be made more meaningful by encouraging self-checking and peer review that are guided by checklists such as the one in the vignette. These direct learners to specific aspects of the written text.

4. Clarify for Yourself and Your Students How Their Writing Will be Evaluated

In Chapter 12, we look in detail at aspects of assessment and evaluation. At this point, however, it is useful to recall what I said in Chapter 1 about the difference between the two terms. 'Assessment' refers to the techniques and procedures for deciding how well learners are doing. 'Evaluation' is a broader term. In addition to determining how well learners have done, it also involves making judgments about why they have performed well on some objectives and not so well on others.

When it comes to assessment, one of the 'buzz phrases' these days is 'assessment *for* learning' rather than 'assessment *of* learning.' Assessment for learning builds assessment into the heart of the teaching learning process, rather than being some-thing that happens at the end of the learning process. Learners as well as teachers have a role to play here and are involved in self-assessment and self-evaluation.

In any kind of assessment/evaluation, it is important that learners are aware of the criteria being used to judge their written work. These criteria need to be made explicit. Are you, the teacher, giving weight to creativity, accuracy of grammar, spelling, and punctuation, use of the imagination, ability to follow the generic structure of a text, or 'all of the above'? If 'all of the above,' are you giving equal weighting to all of the criteria, or giving more weighting to some than others?

What Teachers Want to Know

The focus of this question and answer section is on the relationship between real-world writing tasks and classroom, or pedagogical, tasks.

Question: What are some of the things that we can do in our writing class that reflect the kinds of things that learners want or need to do with writing outside of the classroom?

Response: Think about some of the fundamental reasons for writing in the first place. Why do we write? First, we write to preserve information that might be lost if we didn't have it written down. Second, we write to obtain information. Third, we write to convey information across time and space. Next, and perhaps most importantly from a personal point of view, we write for social purposes. Finally, and this is by no means an exhaustive list, we write as an aid to reflection. You need to think of tasks that learners can complete in their own time, that are authentic. Even better, get learners to think of tasks themselves. Have them list the kinds of writing they do in their own language, and get them to do the same things in English – sending emails, keeping a diary, extending birthday wishes on Facebook – there are lots of possibilities. Get them to the point where writing becomes a habit.

Question: If I ask students to do the writing in their own time, they often just don't do it, so when they turn up for class, there's nothing for me to work with and my lesson plan is ruined.

Response: This is a common problem. Try doing it in stages. For example, give them a guided reflection task to do for the last ten to fifteen minutes of the class. Initially, give them sentence completion prompts such as the following:

> "In today's lesson I learned . . ."
> "I enjoyed . . ."
> "In the next lesson, I would like to . . ."

When they are familiar with this task, get them to do it out of class, and bring their reflective piece to the next class for debriefing. Finally, abandon the prompts and simply ask them to write a 100–150 word reflection on the lesson out of class.

In class, give them a speed-writing assignment. Put them into small groups and have them discuss a topic or issue. If you can come up with a subject that is topical, and perhaps a bit controversial, then that's good. After they have discussed the topic for ten to fifteen minutes, and made notes, tell them to work individually, and to write as much as they can on the topic. Emphasize that you want quantity rather than quality. They don't have to worry about grammar or finding the right word. The have fifteen minutes to write as much as they can. You can make it competitive, if you like. Keep them in their groups, and get them to write individually, then at the end of the period, they each count the number of words they have written and calculate a group tally. The group that has written the most wins. Then they spend the rest of the class drawing on their individual speed-writing efforts to produce a group piece. They polish the piece and then exchange it with another group for a group conference. Using a procedure like this, you are combining both process and product approaches to writing. The students are not spending the entire class writing but they are producing something that can be used as the basis of a productive lesson.

Question: I heard that setting up an email tandem exchange is a good way of encouraging learners to write outside of the classroom. What is an email tandem exchange?

Response: If you have students who are at the right level – intermediate and above – and if you have a connection with a teacher in another country, then tandem email exchanges are an excellent way of getting students to write outside of the classroom. It's a bit like an electronic pen pal system. Two learners who are learning each other's language are paired up through email. For example, Carmen from Bogota is learning English, and Roxanne from Washington is learning Spanish. Carmen writes to Roxanne in English, and Roxanne writes to Carmen in Spanish. They communicate on topics of common interest, and can correct their partner's mistakes and offer suggestions for improving their expression. The feedback will be in the writer's first language – Carmen writing in Spanish and Roxanne writing in English. So not only do they get to produce the target language, but they also receive native speaker models. Learners not only improve their linguistic knowledge, but they also get valuable information about the target culture as well.

TASK

Make a list of the ways in which learners can be encouraged to use the Internet to write in English beyond the classroom.

Use one of these as the basis for creating a 'blended task' in which the task is carried out partly in class and partly out of class.

Step 1: Pre-task: Teacher and students collaborate to prepare for the out-of-class task through one or more schema-building tasks.
Step 2: Task: Students complete task independently out of class.
Step 3: Post-task: In class, learners debrief and receive feedback.

Small Group Discussion

When teaching language, including the teaching of writing, we are also teaching culture. In the extracts that follow, the teacher and students discuss a concept known as contrastive rhetoric. As you read, think about your own examples and experiences with this concept.

TEACHER: During the week, I asked you to read up on contrastive rhetoric. In this discussion thread, I'd like you to address the following questions:
What is contrastive rhetoric?
What examples or experiences can you share in regards to this concept?

JENNIE: I liked what Ula Connor (1996) had to say about the study of contrastive rhetoric being the study of how different languages and cultures have different rhetorical conventions of constructing discourse that are culturally based. When someone writes in their second language, they tend to carry the conventions of their first language over to the second language.

PHIL: I read the Connor article but I didn't quite get the point. Can you give an example?

JENNIE: Yes, well in English speaking cultures, we tend to make our position or argument clear at the beginning of our essay or whatever it is that we're writing, and then give examples to back up our point. Or we make a very clear statement of a problem and then work through to a position on, or a solution to, the problem supporting it with examples or evidence as we go along. In many Asian cultures, they don't do this. They will begin by providing lots of contextual background information, and will kind of circle around the issue or problem. Sometimes, at the end of their writing, they may not even state their position explicitly but leave it up to the reader to infer their proposed solution. For Western readers, this kind of writing sometimes seems unstructured or even pointless.

KIM: I didn't read the Connor article or chapter, but I read what Bob Kaplan (1966) had to say. I read that he was the 'father' of contrastive rhetoric. In the piece I read, he had some nice diagrams to illustrate the ways that different cultures presented a text. So the Western culture was represented as a straight line, like an arrow, shooting in one direction. For Asian cultures, it was a spiral with the issue or solution at the center, and the spiral getting closer and closer to the center.

RICHARD: So does contrastive rhetoric only apply to writing? Wouldn't it also apply to speaking?

TEACHER: You're quite right Richard, it can also apply to spoken language. I had an interesting introduction to contrastive rhetoric when I first went to a business meeting in Japan years ago. In a Western business meeting, there would be an agenda, and as each point came up for discussion, everyone would chime in with their opinion. Sometimes the discussion could get quite heated. In the Japanese context, there was no explicit agenda. The first half of the meeting consisted of the head of the meeting doing all of the talking. He asked lots of what seemed like social questions that had nothing to do with the meeting, and I kept wondering "Are we ever going to get around to the point of the meeting?" Then he got down to business and spoke for a long time as though he was giving a lecture. I found it very strange and very frustrating. But today, we're talking about writing, and that is where the focus is for this discussion.

RICHARD: So, how does contrastive rhetoric apply to the writing classroom?

TEACHER: Would anyone like to share his or her ideas?

JOHN: Maybe the first thing is to make the issue explicit. I'd say that my learners aren't even aware of these differences, so they subconsciously transfer the rhetorical patterns from their first language. The next step would be to give them lots of models of different text types in English, showing them the rhetorical patterns underlying an argumentative text, a problem-solution text, a report, and a narrative. Finally, get them to produce their own texts following the model.

NICOLE: Since I came across the concept of contrastive rhetoric, I make sure that I build it into my writing class. I have heterogeneous language groups from a variety of different first language backgrounds. First of all, I get them to write a paragraph on a particular topic following the cultural format of their own language. Then I get them in small groups of mixed nationalities to discuss the similarities and differences between their different versions. Next I give them examples that have been written by native English speakers. Finally, I get them to rewrite their own paragraph following the rhetorical pattern of English.

Commentary

In this discussion thread, the students discuss the concept of contrastive rhetoric, exploring what it is, and how it can inform the teaching of writing. One student also makes the point that the concept also has implications for certain spoken genres such as a business meeting.

TASK

Summarize the ideas presented in the small group discussion and add three ideas of your own for exploiting the concept of contrastive rhetoric in the writing classroom.

Summary

Content focus	Writing in a second language
Vignette	Scaffold class time on learning – not writing, collaborative peer teaching, personalizing, generic structure of the target text
Issue in focus	The process/product debate
Key principles	1. Understand your students' reasons for writing. 2. Provide many opportunities for your students to write. 3. Make feedback helpful and meaningful. 4. Clarify for yourself and your students how their writing will be evaluated.
What teachers want to know	The relationship between real-world tasks and pedagogical tasks; turning real-world tasks into learning tasks
Small group discussion	Contrastive rhetoric and the place of culture in the writing classroom

Further Reading

Weigle, S.C. (2014) Considerations for teaching second language writing. In M. Celce-Murcia, D. Brinton, and M.A. Snow (eds.) *Teaching English as a Second or Foreign Language.* Boston: National Geographic Learning.

This contribution expands on some of the key themes of Chapter 6, including a discussion of the nature of second language writing, needs-based teaching, the process approach, the pre-task, task, follow-up teaching cycle applied to writing, and the connections between writing and the other skills.

References

Connor, U. (1996) *Contrastive Rhetoric: Cross-Cultural Aspects of Second-Language Writing.* Cambridge: Cambridge University Press.

Kaplan, R. (1966) Cultural thought patterns in intercultural education. *Language Learning,* 16, 1–20.

Nunan, D. (2005) *Go For It Level 2 Students' Book.* 2nd Edition. Boston: Thomson/Heinle.

Nunan, D. (2013) *Learner-Centered English Language Instruction: Selected Works of David Nunan.* New York: Routledge.

Rodrigues, R. (1985) Moving away from the writing-process workshop. *English Journal,* 74, 24–27.

Sokolik, M. (2003) Writing. In D. Nunan (ed.) *Practical English Language Teaching.* New York: McGraw-Hill.

White, R. and V. Arndt (1991) *Process Writing.* London: Longman.

7
PRONUNCIATION

Goals

At the end of this chapter you should be able to:

- differentiate between segmental phonology and suprasegmental phonology
- define the following terms: phoneme, stress, rhythm, intonation, contrastive analysis
- describe strategies and techniques for teaching segmental and suprasegmental phonology
- describe four important principles for teaching pronunciation
- make decisions about which pronunciation features to teach particular student groups

Introduction

When it comes to pronunciation, language teachers can be divided into two groups: those who love teaching it, and those who hate it. Many years ago, when I started teaching, I belonged to the latter group. This probably had something to do with the fact that I had little idea of what I was doing. At the time, I didn't know much about the teaching of vocabulary and grammar either, but I found words, and how they were put together to make grammatical sentences, fascinating. Problems with the teaching of pronunciation are compounded by the fact that in order to teaching pronunciation, you need to know about phonetics and phonology. These subjects are filled with horrifying terms such as phonemes, segmentals, suprasegmentals, bilabial plosives, fricatives, allomorphic variation – the list goes on and on. One other problem had to do with the fact that when I began teaching, the language teaching profession was still dominated by the audiolingual method, which is based on behaviorist psychology and structural linguistics. From behaviorist psychology came the notion that learning was a matter of habit formation. Structural linguistics emphasizes the importance of contrast when analyzing structures in the language.

In this chapter, I will try to keep technical terms to a minimum, although familiarity with some key terms is both necessary and desirable. If you are interested in a little more detail than is provided here, you might like to take a look at my introduction to language (Nunan, 2013). For a book-length treatment of pronunciation, I recommend Celce-Murcia *et al.* (1996).

Two terms that you need to know are 'segmental phonology' and 'suprasegmental phonology.' Segmental phonology has to do with the individual sounds of the language (the phonemes) and the differences in conceptual or semantic meaning brought about by different phonemes. 'Buck' and 'duck' both belong to the animal kingdom, but are very different creatures. One has four legs and fur, the other has two legs and feathers. The words denoting the creatures are identical except for the phonemes /b/ and /d/. Suprasegmental phonology also has to do with contrasts. However, the contrasts here are concerned, not with differences in individual sounds, but with differences in stress, rhythm, and intonation. These signal differences, not of semantic meaning, but of attitudinal meaning.

When I started teaching, the macroskills (listening, speaking, reading, and writing) and language systems (grammar, vocabulary, and pronunciation) tended to be taught separately, rather than being integrated. My initial distaste for pronunciation classes had to do with a teaching technique called minimal pair drilling. The creator of the drill would identify two contrasting phoneme such as 'i' /i/ and 'e' /iy/ as in the words 'ship' and 'sheep' and create a forty-five-minute lesson designed to get the learners to hear the difference between the two sounds, and then to produce them accurately. The learners would have to listen to an utterance such as 'Point to the ship' while the teacher held up two pictures, one of a ship and one of a sheep. They would then have to point to the appropriate picture. This would be followed by a production exercise in which the teacher would say, "Listen and repeat, 'ship,' 'ship'." The students would chant "ship, ship." Then the teacher would say "ship, sheep" and the students were supposed to make the appropriate oral discrimination. I found this mindless repetition excruciating, and those forty-five-minute lessons seemed to go on forever.

Vignette

This vignette takes place in a private language school in Brazil. The teacher is a young, British male who has been teaching for three years. In a previous lesson, the students started on a unit of work which had three main goals:

- understanding descriptions of everyday objects
- understanding vague descriptions
- indicating non-understanding by requesting repetition.

The topic was kitchenware. The students had done various listening, speaking, vocabulary, and grammar tasks involving objects such as a frying pan, chopsticks, corkscrew, cutting board, spatula, can opener, etc.

The teacher turns to the board and writes *What is this called?* He turns back to the class and says, "Listen to me read this question twice. Can you hear the difference between the two times?" He reads the sentence through twice, the first time without any stress and the second time with the stress on 'what.' He then asks, "What was the difference? Lucio?"

Lucio replies, "I have difficult to hear."

"You have difficulty hearing the difference? Did anyone hear the difference?"

One student replies, "The second time 'what' is different."

"Different? How different?"

"The sound is . . ." the student pauses, searching for the right word. "Stronger."

"Stronger," repeats the teacher. "Yes, stronger and louder, and what do we call this?"

"Stress," replies another student.

"Stress, yes, stress. Very good, Patricia. You remembered from last week. So . . . what was the difference in meaning? Why did I stress the question word the second time?"

The students discuss the teacher's question among themselves, and then one of the students says, "Um, because . . ."

"Yes?"

"The first time, is just a question. No stress. Just a question."

"So, what does the person want? The person asking the question?"

"He just want information."

"Information. Right, yes. He just wants information. And the second time?"

"The second time, have the stress on *what*. He not sure what the person want. He want the person to repeat what he have said."

"Good. He wants the person to repeat what he said. So, when the question word is stressed, it's a request for the other person to repeat what they said. He doesn't have to say *Excuse me, could you repeat what you said*. Stress on the wh- word carries that information. OK, good. Now I want you to listen to the example. Listen to the way that this works in a conversation. You can look at the conversation on your worksheet." The teacher plays the following conversation, which is reproduced in their worksheet.

MALE: What is this called?
FEMALE: It's called a cutting board.
MALE: **What** is it called?
FEMALE: A cutting board.

"So," says the teacher. "Did you hear the difference in how 'what' is pronounced?"

"Yes, yes," say the students.

"OK. So now I'm going to find out how good you are. Look at the questions on your worksheet. I want you to put a check mark next to the ones that are requests for the speaker to repeat information. I'll play the tape twice. The first time, just listen. The second time, mark your answers. Ready?"

WORKSHEET

1. What are they called? _____
2. What are these things called? _____
3. What is that on the table? _____
4. What is it used for? _____
5. Who bought that for you? _____
6. Where did you get it? _____

The teacher plays the tape twice. The script is reproduced below.

TAPESCRIPT

Male: What are they called?
Female: **What** are these things called?
Male: **What** is that on the table?
Female: What is it used for?
Male: **Who** bought that for you?
Female: Where did you get it?

"Now, I want you to check your answers with a partner." He gives the students a minute to check their answers, and then gets feedback from the class. He plays the tape a third time so that the weaker students can hear the stressed words again, now that they know what these are.

"Right, now it's your turn. I want you to listen to the questions again. I'll pause the CD after each question, and I want you to repeat. Pay attention to the way that the speaker does or doesn't stress the wh- question word."

The teacher does the choral repetition task twice, and then gets the students into pairs. He says, "OK, now it's time be a little bit creative. I want you to make up your own conversations following the model that we practiced at the beginning of the lesson. Pick one of the questions we just practiced and make a conversation. Let's do one of these together as a class so you're sure of what you have to do. Claudia, pick a question you would like us to work on."

Claudia studies her worksheet and says, "Number five."

"Number five, OK. 'Who bought that for you?' Is this a request for information or a request for the person to repeat what they said?"

"A request to repeat?"

"Exactly, Silvia," says the teacher. "A request to repeat. So how would the conversation begin? Claudia, you wanted to work with this question. How do you think the conversation would begin?"

"Maybe, Who bought that for you? No stress," says Claudia.

"OK, but let's make it a little bit more interesting. How about using one of the words we practiced yesterday? That . . . what? What's a word from yesterday?"

"Who bought that frying pan for you?"

"Good." The teacher writes the question on the board. "And an answer might be?"

"Maybe Jim bought the frying pan for me," says Claudia's partner.

"OK." The teacher writes the answer on the board. "And then, Claudia?"

"**Who** bought the frying pan for you?"

"Great," says the teacher writing the question on the board and underlining the 'who'. "And what would be a good answer?"

"Jim bought the frying pan for me," says Claudia's partner.

"OK. That's correct, but you don't need to say all that. You can just say Jim did." The teacher writes it on the board. "Now you all have a model. You don't have to follow it exactly. Be a bit creative, OK. In fact, *don't* use question five. Use another one. You can write out your conversation, and practice. Then I want you to practice without looking at the conversation. Finally, exchange papers with another pair and practice their conversation. Got it? OK, off you go."

(This vignette is adapted from a lesson based on Nunan, 2003)

REFLECT

What 3 things did you notice in the vignette? Write them down in note form.

1. _____
2. _____
3. _____

My Observations on the Vignette

1. As with a number of other vignettes, the teacher builds on skills and language that had been worked on in previous lessons. This underlines a point that is not always obvious to new teachers. Lessons do not exist as discrete 'packages.' Rather, they flow together as the course evolves.

2. The lesson extract focuses on a suprasegmental pronunciation feature – the use of stress on a wh- question word as a means of requesting repetition.

The pronunciation point was not selected from a prior list of pronunciation features, but was a key linguistic feature of the authentic conversation on which the unit was based.

3. The pronunciation work is preceded by a listening lesson. The instructional sequence thus followed the principle of 'from comprehension to production.' In other words, it begins with comprehension exercises and tasks before moving on to production tasks.

4. The teacher begins the segment by drawing attention to the pronunciation feature. She then gives the learners the opportunity to master the feature through a repetition exercise. In the final phase of the instructional cycle, she adds a creative element, getting the learners to use the feature in a communicative activity, and thus bringing together form and function. She ensures success by scaffolding and modeling what is required in the final creative task.

Issue in Focus: Suprasegmentals

The issue that I wish to put under the microscope in this chapter is that of suprasegmentals. This is because comprehension problems for the listener are more likely to be caused by problems of stress, rhythm, and intonation than by inaccuracies in the pronunciation of individual vowels and consonants. Context can often help when it comes to figuring out meaning when a speaker has mispronounced an individual sound. For example, if you are by the waterfront and a stranger asks, "Excuse me, where is the sheep terminal?" you will naturally assume that they are referring to an ocean-going vessel rather than a fleecy, four-legged mammal.

Celce-Murcia *et al.* provide the following definition of the concept:

> The suprasegmental features [of language] involve those phenomena that extend over one sound segment. [These include] word stress, sentence stress, and rhythm along with adjustments in connected speech (i.e., the adjustments or modifications that occur within and between words in the stream of speech).
>
> *(Celce-Murcia et al., 1996: 35)*

The three aspects of suprasegmental phonology that you need to be familiar with are stress, rhythm, and intonation. These all signal attitudinal meaning. I provide a brief description of each of these along with examples.

Stress refers to the emphasis we give to individual syllables within a word as well as the emphasis given to words within utterances. Emphasis is provided by making a syllable longer, louder, and higher in pitch. In words of two or more syllables, one syllable will be more heavily stressed than the others. For example:

EMphasis
unHEALTHy
exPLAIN

According to Celce-Murcia *et al.* the origin of the language from which a word derives will be an important determiner of word stress. Those words that came into English from German, for example, will tend to have the stress on the first syllable.

Within an utterance, a speaker will emphasize or stress the word that is most important. Most utterances will have what is called an unmarked form. When speakers depart from the expected or unmarked form, they are drawing the listener's attention to the fact that the utterance is performing a function that is different from the expected. We saw a teacher practicing this in the vignette, above. In general, when we ask a question, we want information, and in the unmarked form of the question, the stress will fall on the content word. An example from the vignette is the question 'What's it **called**?' In the marked form the stress falls on the wh- word (**What's** it called?). This changes the function from a request for information to a request for repetition.

Rhythm refers to the way that the alternation of stressed and unstressed syllables within an utterance gives a 'tune' to the utterance. In English, rhythm is important, because the language does not always follow the stressed, unstressed, stressed, unstressed pattern of many other languages. There are utterances that do follow the pattern, for example, 'I **need** to **see** you **now**.' Languages such as Spanish and Chinese, which follow the stressed/unstressed pattern, are called 'syllable timed.' English, which doesn't follow the pattern, is called stressed timed. In stressed timed languages, the unstressed syllables are spoken quickly and squashed together so that the ear is drawn to the important, content words. In an utterance such as 'I was late because of the weather,' the words 'because of the' will occupy approximately the same amount of time as the content words 'late' and 'weather.' Mastering stress timing is a major challenge for speakers of syllable timed languages.

In the preceding paragraph, I used the example 'I **need** to **see** you **now**.' This is the unmarked way of pronouncing the utterance. However, depending on the communicative context, other words can be stressed to signal that they are the important ones. For example:

A: I need to see you now.
B: Who needs to see me now?
A: **I** need to see you now.
A: I need to see you now.
B: Who do you need to see now?
A: I need to see **you** now.

While stress and rhythm refer to the emphasis or loudness given to individual syllables and words, intonation refers to the up and down tones that are produced. Some languages, such as Chinese and Thai, use different tones to signal differences of semantic meaning. In English, rising and falling tones signal differences of attitudinal meaning. Consider the utterance 'That's my drink, isn't it?' spoken with a rising intonation. The rising intonation indicates the speaker's lack of certainty as to whether the drink is his or not. The utterance spoken with a falling intonation signals a very different meaning, namely that the speaker believes the drink to be his but is seeking confirmation.

Emphasizing suprasegmentals at the expense of focusing on the accurate reproduction of individual sounds was stimulated by the development of communicative and task-based language teaching in the 1980s and beyond. This is not to say that focusing on individual sounds was abandoned entirely, but that the emphasis shifted to tasks and activities in the classroom in which the communicative effect of pronunciation was paramount.

Key Principles

1. Begin with Comprehension Before Production

This principle is as important in pronunciation work as it is in any other aspect of mastering a language. It is important because we can't pronounce sounds or other phonological features of a language that we can't discriminate aurally. This is true regardless of the language that we speak. When I moved to Bangkok and started learning Thai, I could only identify a couple of the five tones in Central Thai dialect. I had to spend many hours in a language laboratory listening to tapes before I was able to discriminate aurally between the five tones. It was only when I was able to hear the differences between the tones that I was able to make a start on learning to produce them. Similarly, many Asian speakers have a lot of work to do in order to hear the difference between /l/ and /r/, and if they can't hear the difference, they will never be able to produce the difference.

2. Set Realistic Goals

The goal for the learner should be to speak intelligibly, rather than speaking like a native speaker. (An unrealistic goal as no two native speakers are alike!) When getting learners to practice individual sounds, don't have them produce the sounds in isolation but in connected streams of speech. Goodwin (2014) has this to say on the importance of setting realistic goals:

> For our purposes, *intelligibility* is defined as spoken English in which an accent, if present, is not distracting to the listener. Our goal is not to "fix a broken accent" but rather to promote intelligibility between speakers in a particular context. Since no one accent is dominant in every context, neither teachers nor learners need to sound like idealized native speakers.
>
> *(Goodwin, 2014: 145)*

In considering the principle of intelligibility, we need to decide whether a particular phonemic distinction impedes comprehension. In discussing principle 1, I mentioned the difficulty that many Asian speakers have discriminating between certain sounds in English such as /l/ and /r/. In many situations, the context will make the speaker's communicative context clear, and it therefore doesn't matter whether or not the sounds are discriminated.

3. Teach the Connections Between Form and Function

One of the shortcomings of audiolingualism was that it was based on drills and exercises that focused almost exclusively on form rather than function. In communicative language teaching, the aim is to show learners the relationship between form and function, to demonstrate that we have different forms to express different meanings. As indicated in the preceding section, it was the development of communicative language teaching that led to a shift in focus away from the discrete point teaching of individual sounds to the ways in which stress, rhythm, and intonation allow for the expression of attitudes, feelings, degree of certainty, and so on.

4. Keep Affective Considerations Firmly in Mind

This is a principle put forward by John Murphy (2003) in his excellent overview article on teaching pronunciation. The way we speak is an integral part of our personality. I have a friend who was brought up bilingually in English and French. Although she can speak English with a flawless English accent, she chooses to speak it with a French accent because she has been told it sounds 'cute.' In foreign language situations, schoolchildren are often reluctant to speak because they are embarrassed at making 'funny' sounds in front of their friends. On this matter, Murphy (2003: 110) has this to say:

> Emotions can run high whenever language learners are asked to develop new pronunciation habits. It is essential to realize that pronunciation practice normally takes place in front of other students and a teacher . . . a learner may fear rejection from classmates if her or his pronunciation begins to sound better than other students in the room.

Technology has an important role to play here. There are many software packages and web-based programs that allow students to work on their pronunciation in their own private space where they will not run the risk of being teased by fellow students.

What Teachers Want to Know

In this section, the teacher responds to queries from students about the importance of integrating pronunciation with other skills and systems, and provides advice on deciding what pronunciation items to teach.

Question: Why is it important to integrate pronunciation with other aspects of language such as listening and grammar? Wouldn't it make more sense to teach it separately?

Response: As far as possible, all aspects of language should be integrated. If you teach a particular pronunciation feature in isolation, it makes it more difficult for learners to appreciate the communicative purpose of the feature than if it's taught in context. That doesn't mean we *never* teach items in isolation. However, the pronunciation feature should be presented and practiced in context. The usual sequence is, first, to present the pronunciation feature in context, for example in a conversation or some other listening text. Second, draw the attention of the learners to the feature in question and explain the communicative function of the feature. Third, create an exercise that focuses on the form, for example an exercise to discriminate between minimal pair phonemes such as /t/ /d/ or word stress. Next, get the learners to practice the item. Finally create a communicative exercise such as a role-play to give the learners further practice in context.

Question: How do we decide what pronunciation items to teach?

Response: From a communicative perspective, it's best to select an item that is a key feature of the listening and speaking texts that learners are working with. So the best starting point is not a predetermined pronunciation item, but the texts that are a cornerstone of your teaching materials. You might be teaching a lesson on asking for clarification in which a conversation such as the following interaction occurs.

[The conversation takes place in a noisy restaurant.]

A: Could you pass me the salt, please?
B: Sorry?
A: The salt. Could you pass me the salt?
B: Sorry, I couldn't hear you. It's so noisy. Here you go.
A: Thanks.

The obvious pronunciation point to focus on here is the use of intonation with the word 'sorry' to realize the functions of asking for clarification and apologizing. When asking for repetition, we say 'sorry' with a rising intonation. When apologizing, we use falling intonation. The teaching sequence would be, first, to focus on listening tasks related to the dialogue, or dialogues, then an aural discrimination exercise, and finally a production task. The discrimination exercise might go like this.

Listen to the examples
  Example 1: Asking for repetition. *Sorry?* (rising intonation) *Could you say that again?*
  Example 2: Apologizing. *I'm going to be a bit late. Sorry.* (falling intonation)

Now listen to the conversations. Is the person asking for repetition or apologizing?

1. R A
2. R A
3. R A
4. R A
5. R A
6. R A

Tapescript

1. A: Sorry, I can't make it tonight.
   B: That's OK. Maybe some other time.
2. A: Sorry? What did you say?
   B: I asked what you wanted to order.
3. A: Sorry. I missed the train.
   B: That's OK. I just arrived myself.
4. A: Sorry? Could you repeat that please?
   B: Sure. It's 5556711.
5. A: Sorry? I didn't catch that.
   B: What kind of dressing would you like?
6. A: Sorry. I forgot to bring your book back.
   B: No problem. Just bring it back tomorrow.

(Adapted from Nunan, 2003)

The production task could be a controlled role-play or simulation. These are excellent for practicing stress, rhythm, and intonation in context.

With this approach, you might want to have a checklist of the kinds of pronunciation items that you want your learners to master. Begin with the listening material that is going to form the basis of a lesson or unit of work, and see which of these items occurs in the listening. Then build a listening exercise around it. This is a reversal of the traditional procedure of beginning with an item and writing a dialogue or some other listening text that embodies the item. In other words, to an extent, the texts 'select' the pronunciation items for you.

TASK

Identify a pronunciation feature (either segmental or suprasegmental) in a listening text. Create a pronunciation exercise using the above example as a model.

Small Group Discussion

Many learners begin learning a language with the goal of developing a native-like pronunciation. This issue, along with that of varieties of English, is discussed here by a group of TESOL students.

TEACHER: I want to start this thread by getting you to consider what our goal should be in teaching pronunciation.

CARMEN: Many of my students want to develop a native-like pronunciation, and, of course, they almost always end up being disappointed, because it's just not realistic. I emphasize to them that their goal should be to develop a comprehensible accent – one the other people can understand.

JEFF: When my students say that they want to be able to pass themselves off as a native speaker, I ask them "A native speaker of what?" There are so many varieties of English around the word – English, American, Canadian, Scottish, Welsh, Australian, New Zealand, South African. And even within these, there are huge variations. Someone from the south of England sounds very different from someone from the Midlands, who, in turn, will sound very different from someone from the north.

ALICE: Then there are all of the other varieties of English – Indian English, Philippine English, Singapore English, and so on. When I worked in Singapore, there was a move on the part of the government to stamp out Singapore English, or Singlish, as it was called. In my school, the policy was to encourage the use of standard English in class. There was no way you could 'stamp out' Singlish. The kids thought it was cool, and would tease students who used standard English out of class. Many teachers also used Singlish outside of the formal classroom as a way of bonding with the kids. So in that culture, pronunciation was kind of political.

JANE: I think we need to be aware that people from all over the world have their own English pronunciation. I think it's important that learners are exposed to a variety of pronunciations from around the globe and teachers have to think about who their students are going to use the language with. In the future there will be greater exposure to people from various parts of the globe who use English as the lingua franca. As such the greater the number of different pronunciations learners are exposed to, the better they will be equipped to deal with the variety of people they might meet. Native speakers don't 'own' English, and it's ridiculous to think that they do.

MEI: I agree, but when I show videos of non-native English speakers I get complaints from my students who say they don't want to learn 'poor' pronunciation. I tell them that the vast majority of people they will be communicating with in English will be non-native speakers of English, so they have to learn to understand them. I also tell them that they won't learn other speakers' accents. I also make the point about comprehensibility being the goal – that they are very unlikely ever to develop a native-speaking accent.

TEACHER: What pronunciation differences do you notice in speakers of English from different countries? What implications does this have on the way that we teach English?

JULIANA: In my school, teachers tend to skip the pronunciation lessons because they consider them to be boring. I think this is a mistake. I do a contrastive analysis of the sounds that *don't* exist in the learners' first language. I teach Brazilians, and focus on sounds that don't exist in Portuguese such as voiced and devoiced /th/ as in words such as 'this,' 'that,' 'these,' 'those,' and 'think,' 'thin,' 'thrill.' When pronouncing these words, they tend to use /t/, /f/, /s/. First of all, I get the learners listening in order to discriminate between the sounds. I demonstrate how to form the words. Then, I get them doing minimal pair exercises. I know that these are unfashionable, but they really work for segmental features of language.

TONY: When I teach stress, rhythm, and intonation, etc., I use authentic texts that are fun and that contain the features I want to focus on and use these as the listening. This really helps my students to understand how and why people use these features the way they do. Relating pronunciation to real-life situations and interactions is the approach that works best for me in classes. Students are better able to see the relevance of improving their pronunciation because they realize that they have to get across their intended meaning.

Commentary

This discussion begins with a consideration of the appropriate goal of teaching pronunciation. The participants agree that striving for a native-like pronunciation is unrealistic, and that the goal should be to help the learner achieve a comprehensible accent. In her contribution to the discussion, Juliana tells us that she focuses on those features of English pronunciation that don't occur in the native language of the speakers she teaches. Of course, in order to employ this procedure, you have to be working with a class in which all learners have a common first language.

TASK

Select another language, either one that you are familiar with or one that you are interested in learning about, and do a mini-contrastive analysis. Identify up to six features of English that don't exist in the other language. Create an exercise to practice one of the contrastive items.

Summary

Content focus	Pronunciation
Vignette	Wh- question word stress for repetition
Issue in focus	Suprasegmentals
Key principles	1. Begin with comprehension before production. 2. Set realistic goals. 3. Teach the connections between form and function. 4. Keep affective considerations firmly in mind.
What teachers want to know	Teaching pronunciation in context; deciding on what pronunciation items to teach
Small group discussion	Goals of pronunciation; contrastive analysis

Further Reading

Celce-Murcia, M., D. Brinton and J. Goodwin (1996) *Teaching Pronunciation: A Reference for Teachers of English to Speakers of Other Languages*. Cambridge: Cambridge University Press.

This is my 'go to' book when it comes to getting ideas for teaching pronunciation. I also make sure that it is on the reading list for teacher education courses on teaching pronunciation. The only drawback is that it is based on Standard North American English, and therefore has some limitations if you are teaching other varieties of English.

References

Celce-Murcia, M., D. Brinton and J. Goodwin (1996) *Teaching Pronunciation: A Reference for Teachers of English to Speakers of Other Languages*. Cambridge: Cambridge University Press.

Goodwin, J. (2014) Teaching pronunciation. In M. Celce-Murcia, D. Brinton, and A. Snow (eds.) *Teaching English as a Second or Foreign Language*. Boston: Cengage/National Geographic Learning.

Murphy, J. (2003) Pronunciation. In D. Nunan (ed.) *Practical English Language Teaching*. New York: McGraw-Hill.

Nunan, D. (2003) *Listen In Level 3*. Boston: Thomson/Heinle.

Nunan, D. (2013) *What is This Thing Called Language?* 2nd Edition. London: Palgrave Macmillan.

8
VOCABULARY

Goals

At the end of this chapter you should be able to:

- summarize what is involved in 'knowing' a word
- discuss three strategies for vocabulary acquisition
- describe four important principles for teaching vocabulary
- demonstrate an understanding of word lists, collocation, and lexical phrases
- outline ways in which technology can facilitate the teaching and learning of vocabulary

Introduction

Words matter! They are fundamental to successful language acquisition. In language teaching, this has not always been the case. A key principle of audiolingualism was to limit the teaching of vocabulary so that learners could devote all of their mental energy to mastering the basic grammatical patterns of the language. The argument was that if we were going to strain our learners' brains, it was better to do this by drumming grammar patterns into them than loading them up on vocabulary. Once the patterns were in place, the learners could then 'plug' new words into the appropriate slots in a given sentence pattern.

This argument made sense to me until I went to Italy in the 1970s, and the pressing concern was to communicate immediate needs to the local Italians. (In those days, very few people with whom I interacted in bars, stores, and restaurants spoke English.) In the short term, apart from 'pointing and grunting,' the only way that I could get my needs met was through words. I didn't care about grammar.

Luckily for me, the Italians didn't seem to care much either. So I devoted all of my energy to building up as extensive a vocabulary as I could. Fairly quickly, I found that the best way to learn a new word was within the context of a phrase or a simple sentence, so I began acquiring a rudimentary knowledge of grammar as well.

With the advent of communicative language teaching, the pendulum swung in favor of vocabulary. As I discovered in Italy, it's pretty hard to communicate if you don't have the vocabulary to do so. Since then, words have had their rightful place, alongside sounds and grammar, as one of the three essential subsystems of language.

In a classical collection of articles on the teaching of vocabulary, two eminent applied linguists, Ronald Carter and Michael McCarthy, posed eight fundamental questions that we need to ask ourselves when making decisions about the teaching of vocabulary. Although the book in which they articulated these principles is over a quarter of a century old, the questions remain fundamentally important today.

1. How many words provide a working vocabulary in a foreign language?
2. What are the best words to learn first?
3. In the early stages of learning a second or foreign language, are some words more useful to the learners than others?
4. Are some words more difficult to learn than others? Can words be graded for ease of learning?
5. What are the best means of retaining new language?
6. Is it most practical to learn words as single items in a list, in pairs (for example, as translation equivalents) or in context?
7. What about words which have [several] different meanings? Should they be avoided? If not, should some words be isolated for learning first?
8. Are some words more likely to be encountered in spoken rather than written discourse?

(Carter and McCarthy, 1988: 1–2)

In estimating an individual's vocabulary, we need to decide whether to count individual words or different forms of the same word. Many of the most common words in English have numerous 'relatives' and these are gathered together in word families. Paul Nation provides the example of the word 'agree,' which has twelve closely related family members: agreed, agrees, agreeing, agreement, agreements, disagree, disagreements, disagreeable, disagreed, disagreeing, disagreement, disagrees. If learners acquire all of these variants of 'agree,' do we say that their vocabulary has increased by one word or thirteen?

One of the challenges for someone learning English is that it is very rich lexically. It's actually impossible to give an accurate estimate of the number of words in the English language, because new words are being coined every day, if not every hour. When I was writing a book on language some years ago, I consulted many sources in order to estimate the historical growth and number of words in the language at the time. Estimates ranged from 500,000 to a couple of million. In the end, I fell back on the first 'scientifically' created dictionary in the English language – the *Oxford English Dictionary*.

> [Resources] for creating new words have turned the English language into a lexical leviathan. A thousand years ago, it is estimated, the language consisted of around 100,000 words. Thanks largely to the Norman invasion, French derivatives doubled that number by the end of the Renaissance. In 1928, when the *Oxford English Dictionary* was first published, the number had more than doubled again to something in excess of 400,000 (414,825, to be precise). The recently published online version of the *Dictionary* now contains upwards of 600,000.
>
> *(Nunan, 2013: 45–46)*

Words can be classified in many different ways. One fundamental way is in terms of the grammatical function of the word within a sentence. Is the word functioning as a noun, or as a verb, or even as an adjective or an adverb? A challenge for learners is that many English words can fulfill more than one function. Think of the word 'slide.' It can function as a noun, a verb, or an adjective. (Can you think of sentences in which 'slide' fulfills these three functions?)

Another related distinction that is important when it comes to teaching is between 'content' words and 'function' or 'grammar' words. Content words are those that function as nouns (*dog, book, sky*), verbs (*sit, run, read*), adjectives (*red, beautiful, interesting*), and adverbs (*nicely, now, slowly*). These enable us to refer to entities, events, and states of affairs in the experiential world. Function words don't carry any content but provide the 'glue' that holds a sentence together. They include words such as *the, of, might, however, but*. As we will see, these words can't be taught in isolation but in the context of a sentence.

Vignette

This vignette extract is from a reading class. The students, young adults in an EFL class, are using a popular reading series written by Neil Anderson (2003) called *Active Skills for Reading*. Currently, they are working on Book 2, Lesson 2, which is entitled "Life Expectations." They have completed a reading comprehension exercise based on a text on the topic of the chapter, and are now working on a vocabulary enrichment exercise.

"All right, then," says the teacher, "I want you to turn to page 108. Where we were working yesterday. Got that Lily?"

"Yes," replies Lily.

"OK. Good. Now we are going to do a vocabulary exercise called 'odd word out.' You know this exercise – we've done it before. Look at exercise A." The teacher walks around the room and ensures that all of the students are looking at the correct page. "You see, there are seven groups of words. For each group, you need to circle the word that doesn't belong. You'll see that some of the words are in italics. Don't worry about these for now. These are words from the reading that you did yesterday. I want you to do this exercise individually, and then compare your answers with a partner."

A.

1. *daydream*	imagine	fantasize	make real
2. remember	*look back on*	forget	recall
3. education	hope	*lesson*	learning experience
4. *turn out*	happen	not happen	develop into
5. understand	know	unaware	*realize*
6. at last	*initially*	originally	at first
7. *expectation*	hope	belief	doubt

As the students complete the task, the teacher circulates around the room, dealing with questions and checking the students' responses. She then does a debriefing with the whole class, discussing what similarities and differences there are between the three related items in group 1 – 'daydream,' 'imagine,' and 'fantasize.' She then gets the class into six groups.

"Now," says the teacher, "I want each group to take one group of words. Kenny, you and your colleagues can take group 2, Lily, you take group 3, Lee, group 4, Sammy, group 5, Jo, group 6, and Sandra, group 7. I want you to look up the dictionary definition of the related words in your group, and be prepared to report back to the class on what the words have in common, and what makes them different."

Again, as the students complete their task, the teacher circulates, providing guidance. When all groups have signaled that they have completed the task, the teacher claps her hands to draw the attention of the groups. She then asks each group leader to provide a summary of the conclusions that each group has reached. She then moves on to the next phase of the lesson.

"Now, let's go on to exercise B. What you have to do here is to complete the sentences by putting a word in italics from exercise A in the blanks. You might find that some words can go in more than one space, but you can only use a word once, OK? And make sure that you use the correct form of the word."

"So we have to pick the best word for each blank?" asks Sandra.

"Yes," replies the teacher, "ultimately, there is one best slot for each word, so you have to discuss each of the seven slots before making a final choice. If you have any problems, ask me."

B.

1. Tony didn't _____ that it would take ten hours to drive to Los Angeles from San Francisco. He thought it only took six.

2. When I _____ my childhood, I always remember the summer I spent with my grandmother.

3. _____ we planned to go to the Starlight Room for dinner, but we decided to go to the Sunny Café instead.

4. Living in England has been a good _____ for Monica. She learned more in three months living there than she did in three years of English class.

5. Yoshi, are you _____ about your trip to Europe again? Please try to pay attention in class.

6. It was my _____ that Angela would pass the test, but in the end, she didn't.

7. I didn't think the party would _____ so well, but everyone had a great time.

"OK," says the teacher, "let's go through your responses. The first one, Sammy? Can you give us the first one?"

"Tony didn't *realize* . . ."

"*Realize*, good. Did you all get that? Great. The next one. Grace?"

"*Look back on*" says Grace.

"*Look back on. Look back on.* Excellent. Who wants to do number 3?"

"*Initially.*"

"Thanks Lara. These are too easy. Next time, I'll have to pick a harder exercise."

The students laugh. One says, "No! No! Some are easy, but some are difficult."

"Lily, what did you have for number 4?"

Lily checks her book and says, "*Expectation.*"

"*Expectation?*" The teacher looks around the class. "Does everyone agree?"

"*Lesson.* We picked *expectation* first time, and put *lesson* for number 6, but it didn't seem good."

"No," says the teacher. "It kind of fits, but 'It was my *lesson* that Angela would pass the test' doesn't really work, does it? So, number 4 is *lesson* and number 6 is *expectation*. Excellent Jo. So, how about number 5?"

"*Daydream.*"

"*Daydream?*" repeats the teacher with an upward inflection to her voice, indicating that the student should think again.

"*Daydreaming.*"

"*Daydreaming.* So the last one has to be . . .?"

"*Turn out.*"

"*Turn out.* Good work. So make sure that you add fifteen of the words that you practiced in this lesson to your personal word list. Remember to pick those words that are important or interesting to you."

REFLECT

What 3 things did you notice in the vignette? Write them down in note form.

1. _____

2. _____

3. _____

My Observations on the Vignette

1. The lesson is very much strategy based. The teacher introduces the vocabulary strategy of classifying. In spotting the odd word out, the learners have to group together, or classify, the words that go together. In the process, they distinguish the words that do not belong.

2. By basing the exercise on words from the reading passage that the students had studied the day before, the teacher is reinforcing the words. She is also extending the students' vocabulary range by introducing them to other words and phrases that have meanings similar to the word from the passage.

3. When the students have completed the classification task, she then puts the class into groups and gets them to carry out a dictionary exercise. Using a dictionary effectively is another important learning strategy. Learning when *not* to use a dictionary is, in many ways, just as important as learning when to use one. Some students want to look up every word they don't know. If they are doing an extensive reading exercise, this can interfere with, or even nullify completely, the effectiveness of the extensive reading.

4. In the second part of the exercise, the students get to use the word in context. Learning and consolidating vocabulary by practicing it in context are crucial for building an effective vocabulary base. When reading, guessing the meaning of an unknown word is also an important strategy and a good antidote for

students who want to look up every word in their dictionary. (Of course, their guess may be incorrect, but that can be corrected in a follow-up debriefing session, as the teacher in this vignette does.)

5. At the end of the lesson, the teacher reminds the students to add fifteen words to their personalized word list. This is a good example of the learning strategy of personalization. Each student in the class can select those words that are interesting or relevant to them. By the end of the course, each student will have his or her own personalized word lists. Naturally, there will be some common-alities across word lists, but there will also be items that are unique to particular learners. (For more on strategies for learning vocabulary, see Nunan, 1999.)

Issue in Focus: What Does It Mean to Know a Word?

Answering the question 'What does it mean to know a word?' is not as simple as it might seem. Linguists and textbook writers draw a distinction between receptive and productive vocabulary. A learner's receptive vocabulary consists of those words that he or she can recognize but not use. A productive vocabulary contains those words that a person can both recognize and use.

Knowing a word is not an all-or-nothing issue. There are many English words that I have a partial understanding of, and can use, but struggle to define. Recently, I was asked what the word 'plainsong' meant. I replied that I wasn't entirely certain, but thought that it was a kind of religious singing. It also had the connotation to me of being pretty ancient. Later, I looked up the definition in an online dictionary and discovered that my rather fuzzy understanding was on the right track – more or less. According to the dictionary, 'plainsong' refers to "unaccompanied church music sung in unison in medieval modes and in free rhythm corresponding to the accentuation of the words which are taken from the liturgy." So, you could say that I was on the right track, but my understanding was partial, and even pretty primitive.

Paul Nation is an international expert on the issue of second language vocabu-lary. He argues that a comprehensive knowledge of a word will consist of eight elements:

1. *Meaning*: What does the word mean? Are there multiple meanings? Are there connotations (implied additional meanings)?
2. *Written form*: What does the word look like? How is it spelled?
3. *Spoken form*: What does it sound like? How is it pronounced?
4. *Grammatical behavior*: In what patterns does it occur?
5. *Collocations*: What words are often used before or after the word? Are there certain words we must use with this word?
6. *Register*: Is the word formal or informal? Where can I expect to hear it or use it?

7. *Associations*: How does the word relate to other words? What words could we use in place of this one?
8. *Frequency*: Is this word common? Is it rare? Old-fashioned?

(Nation, 1990: 31)

When teaching vocabulary, we need to be aware of these different dimensions to word knowledge. We must also make decisions about which of these aspects to teach. With beginners, for example, it is unlikely that we would want to teach collocations and associations when first introducing a word. We also need to decide which words to teach for reception and which words we expect learners to be able to make part of their productive repertoire. If you are teaching English for Specific Purposes (for example English for Science, or English for Architects) you may need to teach low frequency vocabulary or words that have a special meaning in the subject concerned. For example, when teaching English for Law, I had to teach the legal meaning of words that students knew in terms of their everyday meaning. (For example 'remedy,' which means a cure or treatment in everyday usage, but means a form of legal reparation in legal register.)

Key Principles

1. Introduce New Vocabulary in Context

In the vignette, we see the teacher consolidating vocabulary encountered in a previous reading lesson by getting the learners to complete a fill-in-the-blank exercise. The value of this rather 'traditional' type of exercise is that it gets the learners identifying an appropriate context for the new vocabulary.

In the introduction, I made the point that when I embark on the learning of a new language, I put a lot of effort, initially, into building up my vocabulary. I'm not too concerned about grammatical correctness, as long as I can get my meaning across. And without vocabulary, this is a serious challenge because my ability to get the things I need is severely restricted, particularly when it comes to information. In the case of physical objects, such as food in a market, it is easier, because I can point to what I want. However, I can't do things like ask the price, or specify the quantity of an uncountable like rice – with oranges, I can raise the requisite number of fingers.

In the early stages of learning a language, I put new words on flashcards. On one side of the flashcard, I write the target word. On the other side, I write the word in a contextualizing sentence. Occasionally, I write the translation in English. I try and use sentences or utterances that are common phrases (called lexical phrases) or conversational routines that are frequently used in casual conversation. That way, I can learn several words at a time. For example, when embarking on the learning of Cantonese, I wanted to learn the word 'gin,' meaning 'to see.' I came across conversational phrases containing the word such as 'Ho loy mh gin' ('Long time, no see'), 'Ting yat gin' ('See you tomorrow'), and 'Yat jun gin'

('See you in a minute'). So not only did I learn the word 'gin,' but also numerous other words such as 'long,' 'time,' 'tomorrow,' 'minute,' and the grammatical negator, 'mh.' Because they came as packaged phrases that I could hear and use frequently, I had little trouble learning the words.

2. Focus on the Most Useful Vocabulary First

Although, to a certain extent, what is useful to one learner may not be useful to another, there is a common core of vocabulary that all learners need. There are the words that are used in a wide variety of spoken and written contexts. Paul Nation (2003) makes the point that:

> The most useful vocabulary that every English language learner needs whether they use the language for listening, speaking, reading, or writing, or whether they use the language in formal and informal situations, is the most frequent 1000 word families in English. The vocabulary is so useful that it covers around 75% of the running words in academic texts and newspapers, over 80% of the running words in novels, and about 85% of the running words in conversations.
>
> *(Nation, 2003: 136)*

It is useful to keep a word list of the 1,000 most common words on hand, and use it as a reference tool. Make sure that you use one that is reasonably up to date. (Not long ago, when writing a textbook, I was given a word list by the publisher that contained the word 'kangaroo,' but not 'computer.' And this was for a textbook for relatively low-proficiency learners!) These lists can be easily found online, and some recommended links are provided later in the chapter.

3. Teach Learners Strategies for Vocabulary Acquisition so that They Can Continually Add to Their Repertoire

One of the themes running through all of the chapters in this book is the importance, not only of teaching language, but also teaching learning strategies.

In the vignette you saw a lesson that was very much strategy based. The teacher introduced three important vocabulary strategies: classifying, using a dictionary, and practicing words in context.

This is so important that I have devoted an entire chapter (Chapter 11) to the topic. It is also particularly important for learners to develop effective vocabulary learning strategies. As we have already pointed out, with hundreds of thousands of words, English is a vocabulary rich language. We cannot possibly teach our learners all the words they will need in order to be effective communicators. Adding new words to our repertoire is a lifelong process for both native speakers as well as second language learners. Learners will need to go on acquiring new vocabulary long after they have left the classroom.

It is therefore crucial that we help equip them with the skills for independent language learning.

4. Pay Attention to Repetition and Spacing

Repetition is important for vocabulary learning. It is rare, although not completely unknown, for a word to be acquired on a single encounter. It happened to me once when learning Cantonese. I was out with a Cantonese friend when, unexpectedly, it started to rain. My friends shouted 'lok yu' and we both ran for shelter. I never needed any repetition of the word in order to acquire it! A rule of thumb is that learners need ten to twenty repetitions of a word in different contexts in order to learn the words. And keep in mind that knowing a word is an incremental process and involves at least eight different aspects of the word. Each repetition should involve acquiring a different feature of the word.

Spacing is also important. Educational psychologists use the phrase 'distributed learning' to capture this aspect of learning. Distributing new learning over time rather than trying to achieve learning all at once will result in more effective learning. So, if the task for the learners is to acquire ten to fifteen new words, they will be acquired more effectively if you devote four sessions of fifteen minutes to the task rather than a sixty-minute session on a single day. As Zimmerman (2014: 292) says: "It is not only the number of times that one encounters a word that is important to learning, but also the spacing between the repetitions."

What Teachers Want to Know

Collocation, lexical phrases, and word lists are the focus of teachers' concerns in this section. These concepts are clarified and practical ways of using them in teaching vocabulary are discussed.

Question: I'm not quite clear about collocation. I've seen it described in various ways. Can you say something about it?

Response: There are different kinds of collocation. The linguist Michael Halliday argues that what he calls lexical collocation is one of the aspects of language that differentiates a coherent text that 'hangs together' from a random collection of sentences. Lexical collocation occurs when two or more words are related semantically. Consider the following conversation.

MARY: How was your weekend?
TOM: It was great. I spent the weekend in the garden.
MARY: I didn't know you were a gardener.
TOM: Yes, I'm a keen gardener. On Saturday I put in some plants – roses, camellias, and azaleas. On Sunday, I planted a couple of fruit trees – a peach tree and an orange tree.

MARY: It sounds as though you were busy.
TOM: I sure was!

This conversation 'hangs together' because it's about a coherent topic – what Tom did on the weekend. One of the things that holds the conversation together is lexical collocation. Several lexical chains run through the conversation. (These are called 'chains' because they form semantic networks running through the conversation and tie the utterances together thematically.)

> week, weekend, Saturday, Sunday
> garden, gardening, gardener
> plants, planting
> plants, roses, camellia, azalea
> fruit tree, peach tree, orange tree

There are other examples of lexical collocation in the conversation, but the above example should give you a clear idea of what collocation is and how it works. What on the surface appears to be a simple conversation turns out to be quite complex.

Collocation is also used to refer to words that commonly co-occur, for example adjective + noun combinations. There are lots of these in English, such as 'mountainous waves.' In fact they, too, are so much a part of the fabric of the conversation that we only notice them when a non-native speaker gets it wrong and says something like "The boat survived the hilly waves." These combinations present a challenge for learners because they are conventionalized ways of speaking and are based on metaphors. They can't be arrived at through logical analysis, but have to be learned over time. There is no reason why we couldn't, or shouldn't, say 'hilly waves' to describe waves that are somewhere between smooth and very rough – we just don't.

Question: What are some practical techniques for teaching collocation?

Response: There are lots of techniques you can use. One would be to get students, preferably working in pairs or small groups, to study a conversation such as the one above or some other written text, and identify the cohesive chains. These can be highlighted by different colored highlighting pens. In the above conversation, orange could be used to highlight the time words, and green could be used for words to do with gardens and gardening. An extension activity would be to get students to extend the networks:

Add more words to the lists

> *Plants*: rose, camellia, azalea.....................
> *Trees*: fruit trees, flowering trees.....................
> *Fruit trees*: peach tree, orange tree.....................

This particular activity can lead into a discussion of hyponyms and hypernyms. A hyponym is a subordinate of a more general concept, so 'rose' and 'camellia' are hyponyms of 'plant.' 'Peach tree' is a hyponym of 'fruit tree,' which is a hyponym of 'tree.' Hypernym is the term for the more general word.

Question: Can you say more about the idea of learning words in lexical phrases rather than learning isolated words?

Response: Lexical phrases are a kind of collocation in that they consist of set commonly occurring expressions such as 'to coin a phrase,' 'in a nutshell,' and 'see you later.' In fact, nothing has been coined, the nutshell contains nuts, not whatever one is talking about, and the speaker has no intention of seeing the other person later. Idioms such as 'it costs an arm and a leg' can also be considered lexical phrases, as can expressions such as 'Would you like to . . .?' and 'Do you mind if I . . .?' These can be taught as formulaic chunks, which learners can memorize. They facilitate the learning process and help beginning and intermediate students increase their spoken fluency. As we have noted already, when teaching formulaic language, or any vocabulary for that matter, it is important that it is presented in meaningful contexts as the context should help with making the meaning more salient and this will facilitate the teaching and learning processes.

Question: What are word lists and how can they be used to teach language?

Response: Word lists consist of the most frequent words in a language. They are usually listed in descending order, from the most to the least frequent items, although they can also sometimes be listed in alphabetical order with their ranking indicated in brackets. Not surprisingly, the most common words are function, or grammar words, such as articles, prepositions, and pronouns, not content words. For example, the twenty most frequent words in English are as follows.

1. the
2. of
3. to
4. and
5. a
6. in
7. is
8. it
9. you
10. that
11. he

12. was
13. for
14. on
15. are
16. with
17. as
18. I
19. his
20. they

The first content words appear as items 30 and 31. These are 'hot' and 'word' respectively. Of course, these word lists have to be updated. Grammar words don't change, but content words do, as do their meanings. (Think of words such as 'twitter,' an ancient word whose contemporary meaning is related metaphorically to its original meaning, but now means short text messages.)

When teaching, we need to take into consideration usefulness as well as frequency. Nation (2003: 135) points out that some words are more useful than others because they have a greater range of functions. For example, 'help' "can be used to ask for help, to describe how people work with others, to describe how knowledge, tools, and materials can make people's work easier and so on." For beginners, the word 'advertise' is much less useful.

In addition to common word lists, there are also academic word lists. These include the words that students studying academic subjects at school and university will need to know.

TASK

Select a short text and analyze it for the collocations it contains. Create an exercise or number of exercises to teach the collocations.

Small Group Discussion

Technology is an integral part of our everyday lives. It plays an important part in our professional lives. It is difficult to imagine developing, teaching, and evaluating courses without the aid of technology. In this discussion, students share their ideas about technology and vocabulary teaching.

TEACHER: Lydia, you said you'd found some word lists on the web. Could you share them with the group?

LYDIA: Sure. There are quite a few available, actually. When you choose one, you need to take various factors into consideration. These include the learner's age, their proficiency level, their purposes for learning the language, the macroskill being focused on and soon.

SARAH: Why is macroskill important?

LYDIA: Because spoken language and written language are different – the grammar is different and the vocabulary is different. Most of the word lists are based on an analysis of written language, but if you're teaching spoken language you should probably take a look at a word list based on spoken language.

There's a wide variety of lists available on the web. If you just want a list of the 1,000 most frequently used words in written texts, check out http://www2.newton.k12.ma.us/~alla_mantsur/1000%20words.pdf. If you're teaching young kids, there a really good word list called the Dolch word list (http://www.mrsperkins.com/dolch.htm), which lists the 220 most common words in children's reading books along with ninety-five additional nouns. The words are in alphabetical order, rather than frequency of occurrence, which is helpful. This list is helpful because it contains common sight words and therefore provides a good basis for early reading. The list might be a bit out of date now, because it was developed quite a long time ago. Also remember that web links are unstable – they can disappear suddenly and without warning!

JIM: Can you tell us what you mean by a sight word, Lydia?

LYDIA: According to the website, sight words are those that can't be sounded out phonetically, but have to be memorized by sight. Apparently about 70 percent of the most common words are sight words. A word like 'big' can be sounded out, but a word like 'could' has to be learned by heart.

I also found some other interesting word list sites, such as one for parts of speech. Here's one for adjectives, for example: http://www.eslgold.com/vocabulary/common_adjectives.html.

You can also look for lists based on themes, such as family, health, etc. For an example of a list based on themes, check out http://www.manythings.org/vocabulary/lists/c/.

Another example of a theme-based list focusing more around the skill of listening is at http://www.esl-lab.com/vocab/. Depending on your learners' purposes for learning the language, you might also want to check out more specific lists, such as an academic word list (i.e. http://www.victoria.ac.nz/lals/resources/academicwordlist/).

As I mentioned, one of the problems with links is that they can easily go 'dead' on you. If that happens to any of the links that I just shared with you, then you can find similar lists through Google or some other search engine. That's how I found these.

TEACHER: That's very helpful, Lydia. Sarah, you were going to research the topic of online corpora and its relevance for vocabulary teaching. What did you find out?

SARAH: Well, a corpus is a large database of language that is put on a computer and can be analyzed in different ways. The early corpora were generally of written language, but these days there are corpora of spoken language as well. Linguists use concordancing programs to compare and contrast spoken and written language as well as to identify patterns in the usage of particular words as well as the most common functions of a word. This can help us make decisions about which functions we should teach first when we're introducing a new word.

VAN: Can you give us an example?

SARAH: I found Michael McCarthy's (1996) book on spoken language to be really useful, with lots of examples. One example he talks about is the verb '*got.*' The database shows that this is basically a spoken form in that it's fourteen times more frequent in spoken than in written language. He says that the most frequent use of '*got*' is to indicate possession, which is not really surprising. But I also read that '*got*' is most frequently associated with accidents, often of a violent nature. It seems that you're more like to encounter '*got*' with '*robbed*,' '*mugged*,' '*stranded*' than with '*lucky*' or '*rich*,' although it also collocates with these words as well.

Commentary

In this discussion list, the students discuss two technological tools that can be readily found on the Internet: word frequency lists and concordancing programs. Both deal with frequency of occurrence, although concordancing programs are probably more powerful in that they contain much more information than simply documenting frequency of occurrence.

TASK

Explore one or more concordancing programs. (Some of these require a subscription, but others are offered free of charge.)

A good example would be the British National Corpus www.natcorp. ox.ac.uk, which provides an online tutorial as well as a simple search function. Find out more about the corpus and how it can be used. Do a simple search for words and common collocations and explore the ways they are used in authentic texts.

If you have more advanced students, get them using this and other corpora to carry out their own independent exploration of new words.

Summary

Content focus	Teaching vocabulary
Vignette	Strategies for vocabulary acquisition
Issue in focus	What does it mean to know a word?
Key principles	1. Introduce new vocabulary in context.
	2. Focus on the most useful vocabulary first.
	3. Teach learners strategies for vocabulary acquisition so that they can continually add to their repertoire.
	4. Pay attention to repetition and spacing.
What teachers want to know	Word lists
	Collocations
	Lexical phrases and formulaic language
Small group discussion	Technology and vocabulary teaching

Further Reading

Zimmerman, C. (2014) Teaching and learning vocabulary for second language learners. In M. Celce-Murcia, D. Brinton, and M.A. Snow (eds.) *Teaching English as a Second or Foreign Language*. Boston: National Geographic Learning/Cengage.

This chapter covers all of the basics of teaching and learning second language vocabulary in a clear and comprehensible way. It has particularly useful sections on practical classroom techniques and well as strategies that learners can apply outside the classroom for increasing their vocabulary.

References

Anderson, N. (2003) *Active Skills for Reading Students' Book 2*. Boston: Heinle.

Carter, R. and M. McCarthy (1988) *Vocabulary and Language Teaching*. London: Longman.

McCarthy, M. (1996) *Spoken Language and Applied Linguistics*. Cambridge: Cambridge University Press.

Nation, I.S.P. (1990) *Teaching and Learning Vocabulary*. Boston: Heinle & Heinle.

Nation, I.S.P. (2003) Vocabulary. In D. Nunan (ed.) *Practical English Language Teaching*. New York: McGraw-Hill.

Nunan, D. (1999) *Second Language Teaching & Learning*. Boston: Heinle & Heinle.

Nunan, D. (2013) *What Is This Thing Called Language?* 2nd Edition. London: Palgrave Macmillan.

Zimmerman, C. (2014) Teaching and learning vocabulary for second language learners. In M. Celce-Murcia, D. Brinton, and M.A. Snow (eds.) *Teaching English as a Second or Foreign Language*. Boston: National Geographic Learning/Cengage.

9

GRAMMAR

Goals

At the end of this chapter you should be able to:

- state how functional grammars differ from formal grammars, and how reproductive tasks differ from creative tasks
- distinguish between prescriptive and descriptive grammars
- outline the advantages and disadvantages of deductive and inductive approaches to the teaching of grammar
- create tasks based on techniques such as grammar dictation
- describe four important principles for teaching grammar
- summarize the arguments for and against conscious learning and subconscious acquisition

Introduction

In the last chapter, I pointed out that the status of vocabulary within the English language curriculum was anything but stable. In the heyday of audiolingualism, it was forced to play a secondary role to grammar, but was reinstated as an equal partner once communicative language teaching came into ascendency. Interestingly, with the advent of communicative language teaching, grammar was similarly challenged. Two versions of CLT developed: the strong view and the weak view. The strong view argued that the explicit teaching of grammar is unnecessary, that learners will 'pick up' the grammar subconsciously when they engage in communicative language learning tasks (Krashen, 1981, 1982). The weak view is that the explicit teaching of grammar is helpful to second language acquisition (Doughty and Williams, 1998). Although the strong view is still popular in some quarters, these days, the consensus is firmly in favor of the weak view.

So, what is grammar? In my 2013 book, I argue that there are two aspects to the definition:

> The first is that grammar has to do with how words are formed, and the second is that grammar is all about how words are combined to form sentences. The academic study of word formation is called morphology . . . while the study of ordering and combining words is called syntax.
>
> *(Nunan, 2013: 63)*

The basic building block of grammar is the clause. There are seven basic clause types. These are described below along with examples.

Clause type	Example
Type 1: Subject + Verb	Maria + sang
Type 2: Subject + Verb + Object	William + saw + a UFO
Type 3: Subject + Verb + Complement	I + became + wary
Type 4: Subject + Verb + Adverbial	I + 've been + in the office
Type 5: Subject + Verb + Object + Object	Malcolm + bought + his wife + a diamond
Type 6: Subject + Verb + Object + Complement	We + think + traditional grammatical analysis + is rather pointless
Type 7: Subject + Verb + Object + Adverbial	We + had to take + our relatives + home

(Adapted from Nunan, 2005: 4)

Grammarians distinguish between prescriptive grammars and descriptive grammars. Prescriptive grammars lay out what is grammatically correct and incorrect, while descriptive grammars articulate what people actually say. You might find it strange that we make this distinction. However, English is ever-changing, and people constantly break prescriptive rules. Think about the rule for countable and uncountable nouns. The prescriptive rule is that we use 'fewer' with countable nouns, and 'less' with uncountable nouns. Thus, we say "There are fewer people going to the movies these days" and "Doctors say we should eat less salt." Well, guess what? Only yesterday, I heard a commentator on television assert that, "There are less people going to the movies these days." In fact, the use of 'less' with countable nouns is becoming increasingly common. (Interestingly, I have yet to hear anyone say "Doctors say we should eat fewer salt.") The challenge for descriptive grammarians is to come up with an explanation for the use of 'less' with countable nouns.

There are two basic approaches to the teaching of grammar: the first is a deductive approach; the second is an inductive approach. I put these approaches under the microscope in the 'issue in focus' section. In the deductive approach, the teacher explains the rule and then gives the learners exercises to apply and consolidate the rule. In an inductive approach, learners study samples of language containing a particular grammatical rule and have to figure out the rule.

Vignette

This vignette is based on a popular technique for reinforcing previously introduced grammar points. It is called grammar dictation, or 'dictogloss.' The technique is relatively simple. The teacher reads a short text at near normal speed. Students jot down key (content) words and then work together in small groups, pooling their resources to reconstruct the text. Grammar dictation is one of my favorite activities because it presents grammar within a communicative context, it requires learners to be actively involved in their learning, it can be used with learners at all levels of proficiency from beginner to advanced, and it can be used with mixed level groups.

The class taking part in this lesson is a group of intermediate level secondary school students. Some of the students have had limited experience with the grammar dictation technique. However, there are several new students in the class who haven't encountered the technique before, so the teacher begins the class by going over the procedures.

The teacher begins by writing 'grammar dictation' on the whiteboard. He turns back to the class and says, "OK, so today, we're going to do a grammar dictation. Do you remember how to do grammar dictation, Kim? We haven't done one for a while."

"Kind of," says the student.

"Kind of. Hmm." The teacher pauses, "Well, just to remind you, I'm going to read you a short passage." He holds up a book containing the passage and waves it at the class. "And, I'm going to read it twice. The first time I read it, I want you to just to listen. Listen for the meaning, and to get a general idea of the story. Then the second time I read it, I want you to write down key words. So are you going to write down the little grammar words, Eun-ha, like '*the*,' '*to*,' '*in*'? Are they key words?"

"No," says the student.

"Good," says teacher. "You're right. These are grammar words. They're important, but I don't want you to write them down. Later you'll need to come up with these words yourself. Write down the key content words individually. Then, in groups, I want you to share your words and reconstruct, or reproduce, the story. Appoint one person – someone who's a good writer, to be the scribe. When you've finished, compare your version with another group and see how similar they are."

A student raises her hand, and the teacher says, "Yes, Erika?"

"Do we have to write the, write the . . ." She pauses, struggling to express herself.

"Write the . . .?" asks the teacher encouragingly.

"The exact words?" says the student.

"No," says the teacher, "you don't have to be exact, but you have to try and get as close as you can. The group that gets the closest to the original version will be the winner."

Several students in the class laugh.

The teacher continues, "But first of all, look at these words." On the board, he writes: 'disaster,' 'Scrabble,' 'not feeling too good.'

"Do you all know these words?"

"What is Scrabble?" one student asks.

"Oh, it's a kind of board game. I thought you all knew Scrabble. You have to make words from letters of the alphabet that are printed on little tiles."

"Oh, yes, we played it one time," says another student.

"We played it last semester, I'm sure," says the teacher. "Well maybe not all of you."

"Not feeling too good?" asks another student.

"Feeling a bit sick," says the teacher. "Not terrible, but not very well. All right, these are some of the words you will hear. So you don't have to write then down. I'll leave them on the board. Now, if you're ready . . ." He picks up the book from which he is about the read the passage and says, "I'll read the text the first time. And . . . And what are you going to do?"

"Listen. Just listen," say several students.

Teacher nods. "Just listen. Right."

The teacher reads the text at near normal speed while the students listen. He then says, "OK, now I'm going to read it again. Listen and write down the words you hear. Remember, just write down key words." He then reads the text a second time. While he does so, the students scribble furiously on their sheets of paper.

TEXT

My weekend was a disaster. I had to change all my plans. On Saturday afternoon I was going to watch football, but my grandmother turned up. So I stayed home and played Scrabble with her. On Saturday night, I was going to go to the movies, but I had to help my dad move furniture. Then on Sunday, I was going to work on a science project with a friend, but he didn't show up. He called and said he wasn't feeling too good. So I played basketball with my brother.

When he has finished, he pauses, giving the students time to finish jotting down words. Then he says, "All right, in groups of four, I want you to work together to reconstruct the story. First of all, decide who is going to write it down then help him or her. Off you go."

The students arrange themselves into groups and begin reconstructing the text. When they have finished, the teacher has them exchange their reconstructions with another group and compare drafts. He then projects the original onto the white-board, and gets them to compare it to the version that they have produced. The lesson ends with a review of the future in the past – the main tense in the passage.

REFLECT

What 3 things did you notice in the vignette? Write them down in note form.

1. _____
2. _____
3. _____

My Observations on the Vignette

1. Learning is collaborative. The students work together in small groups and pool their resources to reproduce the original text. One of the benefits of the grammar dictation task is that all learners are expected to contribute to the completion of the task. In the course of completing the task, they are engaged in authentic communication.

2. The main target structure to be revised is 'future in the past' – *was going to*. The structure is presented in a naturalistic text rather than as isolated sentences, so that the purpose for the grammatical form is clear to the students. It is also integrated with a range of other forms including the simple past, and conjunctions.

3. The task stimulates students to activate their grammatical knowledge of a range of structures, as they are reconstructing the original texts by working with content words. They have to provide the function or grammar words that are the 'glue' holding the sentences together. These include such grammatical items as articles ('the', 'a/an'), prepositions ('on'), pronouns ('I', 'he'), possessives ('my'), etc.

Issue In Focus: Deductive Versus Inductive Approaches to Teaching Grammar

In this chapter, the issue I wish to focus on is deductive versus inductive learning. As indicated in the introduction, in a deductive lesson, the teacher provides the learners with a rule and then gives them exercises in which they apply the rule. In other words, the focus is first on principles, and then on examples. This approach to instruction has dominated Western education from the time of the Greek philosopher Aristotle to the Middle Ages (Cohen and Manion, 2007). At that time, the philosopher Francis Bacon suggested an alternative, looking at examples, and from them, formulating principles. In a grammar lesson the teacher could implement this principle by giving learners samples of language containing a grammatical structure and getting them to figure out the rule.

In some ways, inductive learning is a more 'natural' approach to learning. As we grow up, most of the learning we do outside the classroom involves induction. As children, we observe parents and others who are more skilled than we are, draw conclusions and derive principles based on what we see, and then try them out for ourselves. In traditional societies that don't have formal educational systems, this is the way that learning happens. For example, in Australian aboriginal societies, children learn the ways of their culture by observing and imitating their elders.

So, which is preferable, deduction or induction? The answer is 'it depends.' Neither is inherently superior to the other, and both are complementary. In my own teaching, I tend to favor inductive learning because I believe that having to figure something out for ourselves stimulates a greater depth of processing than simply having it told to us. As one teacher said to me, "When I tell my students something, it goes in one ear and out the other. But, if I get them to work it out for themselves, they remember." As we will see when we look in greater detail at learning styles and strategies, there is evidence that some students learn more effectively through a deductive approach, while others appear to learn more effectively inductively.

Mouly (1978) has suggested that learning is a process of shuttling back and forth between induction and deduction. He argues that as we learn, we use one approach then the other, first working inductively, observing and hypothesizing, and then switching to deductive learning, seeing whether the implications of the hypothesis are borne out in actuality. Deduction thus provides us with a way of validating the hypothesis that we have developed through induction.

Although Mouly's observations on the interrelationship between inductive and deductive reasoning were made to describe the process of scientific investigation, it is easy to see how they can capture processes of learning in the grammar classroom where there is a back-and-forth movement between grammatical rules and language data in the form of texts, sentences, and utterances.

Each of these approaches has pros and cons. Deductive approaches get straight to the point, thereby saving class time. They are also in line with the expectations of students in many learning contexts – they come into the classroom expecting to be told. On the other hand, certain learners, particularly younger ones, may not get the point, particularly if the explanation is clothed in grammatical terminology. It also encourages the belief that language learning is simply a matter of learning the rules of that language.

The advantages of inductive approaches are that they stimulate a greater depth of processing, which makes learning more meaningful and memorable. Students are active constructors of their own learning rather than passive recipients of the teacher's wisdom. It fosters independent learning skills, and, if tasks are carried out collaboratively in the target language, learners actually get practice in using the language authentically while learning it. On the other hand, inductive learning takes more time – figuring something out for ourselves takes more time than being told. The students may also reason their way to a wrong conclusion. Induction also places a greater burden on the teacher because the lesson is less teacher controlled than in a deductive classroom. Finally, it can be frustrating for students who have been conditioned, through prior learning experiences, to expect the teacher to tell them everything. (For an excellent discussion of the pros and cons of deductive and inductive approaches to the teaching of grammar, see Thornbury, 2000.)

Key Principles

1. Integrate Both Inductive and Deductive Approaches into the Teaching of Grammar

As I pointed out in the preceding section, in a deductive instructional sequence, the teacher provides a grammatical explanation or articulates a rule and then gives students a set of exercises that are intended to help the learner master the point. The principle comes first and the examples follow. In inductive learning, the instances come first, in the form of texts or sentences in which the grammatical feature is embedded, and the learners, through a process of guided discovery, come to an understanding of the principle or rule.

Most teachers have their own preferences when it comes to adopting a deductive or an inductive approach. I've revealed my own bias. I favor inductive learning, although there is no solid evidence that it is more effective than a deductive approach for all learners in all situations. My bias is partly ideological, and partly based on research from the field of educational psychology. The ideological roots of my bias stem from my belief in a humanistic approach to life in general, and a constructivist view of education. I believe that learners construct their own learning and knowledge based on a range of input, including deductive input from the teacher. From educational psychology, there is evidence that we do not receive messages in the same shape and form as they are transmitted. We are not walking MP3 recorders! We interpret what we see or hear in the light of our pre-existing knowledge and biases. In addition, teaching experience has shown me time and time again that the more actively a learner processes input the more effectively he or she will learn.

Ultimately, we need to take our bearings from our learners. Some will be naturally inclined toward a deductive approach, preferring to have an understanding of the small bits that make up the language before assembling the language itself. Others will prefer to jump right in and figure things out for themselves. Then, if you are working with young learners, you may have no choice but to adopt an inductive approach. There is no point in giving abstract explanations to young learners. Rather, you need to draw their attention to patterns in the language that they can internalize inductively through games, songs, and chants involving lots of repetition of the target structure.

2. Use Tasks that Make Clear the Relationship Between Grammatical Form and Communicative Function

One of the problems with 'traditional' approaches to grammar is that they present learners with grammatical rules that show how the particular feature is formed, but not how a given form is used to express particular meanings. A commonly cited example is the passive voice. The usual way in which the passive voice is introduced is to show how an active voice sentence is transformed into passive voice. For example, a sentence such as "The dog bit the man" is transformed into "The man was bitten (by the dog)" by making the object of the active voice sentence the subject of the passive voice sentence. Here, while students learn to form the passive from the active sentence, there is no information about *why* we have the passive voice form. The question, "What is the communicative function of the passive voice?" goes unanswered. In fact, the passive voice has a number of communicative functions: to place the emphasis on the recipient rather than doer of the action, when we don't know who performed the action and so on.

3. Focus on the Development of Procedural Rather than Declarative Knowledge

This principle raises the issue of what it means to know something. Procedural knowledge is sometimes known as 'knowing how' knowledge, while declarative knowledge is referred to as 'knowing that' knowledge. A statement such as "I know that when I'm making statements in third person singular, I have to put an 's' on the end of the verb" is an example of declarative knowledge. Actually putting an 's' on the end of the verb when making third person declarative statements in a conversation would be an example of procedural knowledge. The assumption in traditional approaches to grammar was that declarative knowledge would 'turn into' procedural knowledge with practice. However, the two types of knowledge are quite different. All of my students in Hong Kong can spout the rule for what to do with the verb in third person declarative statements. However, more often than not, they leave off the 's' when making such statements.

What is important in teaching grammar is to keep your eye firmly on the goal of developing procedural knowledge, that is, the ability of the students to actually use the grammatical feature accurately and appropriately. If giving them declarative knowledge assists them to do this, then incorporate that knowledge into your teaching, but don't assume that because they know the rule they will be able to use it. Interestingly, the audiolingual method eschews declarative knowledge and argues for an exclusive focus on procedural knowledge. "Learning by analogy, not analysis" is one of the catchcries of the method.

4. Encourage Learners to Use Language Creatively Rather than Reproductively

Reproductive language exercises are those that engage learners in reproducing and manipulating grammatical structures provided by the teacher or the materials they are working with. Essentially, these exercises are designed to give learners practice at mastering grammatical forms. Fill-in-the-blank exercises, sentence matching, listening, and repeating are all examples of reproductive language work. Creative language tasks, on the other hand, require learners to use language authentically. They have to come up with their own utterances, not those provided by the teacher. The grammar dictation task is a good example of a task that requires learners to use language creatively.

Pennington (1995: vi–vii) captures the essence of creative language work when she says:

> In [my] view, grammar is more a matter of selection than correction. Grammar is, in other words, about selecting the appropriate option(s) from a range of possibilities rather than simply recalling and producing – or reproducing – language in one particular form, that is, the one prescribed by the grammar teacher or another authoritative source. Because from this perspective, grammar is a process of choosing forms and constructing language to respond to communicative demands, it essentially involves the learner's creative response to context and circumstance.

What Teachers Want to Know

In this section, the concept of functional grammar is discussed. The other main point covered is the notion that developing the ability to use language creatively is fundamental to language acquisition.

Question: I heard someone talking about 'functional' grammar. Can you tell us what a functional grammar is?

Response: Grammatically, there are two ways of looking at language: as form and as function. Formal grammar has to do with how words are formed and put together. Functional grammar has to do with how different ways of putting words together enable us to make different kinds of meaning.

Traditional approaches to grammar begin with the different word classes – subject, verb, object, complement, adverbial – and how these are combined to make up different clause types. One of the problems with this traditional way of looking at grammar is that it focuses on form but pays insufficient attention to the functions that different grammatical forms have in use. Let me provide an example. The traditional way of introducing the passive voice is to provide learners with a list of active voice sentences, then demonstrate how we transform these sentences by making the object of the active sentence the subject of the passive sentence and changing the tense of the verb. Students are then given practice in transforming active sentences into passive ones. The hidden message in an exercise such as this is that active voice and passive voice are alternative ways of saying the same thing. The formal transformation doesn't provide any insights for the learner as to the communicative function of the passive form.

Functional grammars, on the other hand, seek to show the systematic relationship between form and function. By moving the object to the front of the sentence, we are making it more prominent. In "The council banned private cars from the city during the parade" the focus is on the council. In the passive form, "Private cars were banned from the city during the parade," the focus is on 'private cars.' The passive voice also helps us out when we simply don't know the performer of the action. "Last night, the million dollar lottery was won for the second time this year" sounds less clumsy than "Someone won the million dollar lottery last night. It's the second time this year that someone has won the lottery."

Question: Can you say more about the concept of creative language use?

Response: I draw a distinction between reproductive and creative language use. Reproductive language occurs when learners are given a model sentence or question which they reproduce in the course of completing a task. For example, the students might be doing a survey on likes and dislikes. They have to go around the class asking and answering the question "Do you like . . .?" they then have to report their findings back to the class. "Sally likes ice cream but she doesn't like chocolate." There is a communicative dimension to the task, because the students are exchanging meanings. However, they are basically reproducing and manipulating a target structure, or a limited number of target structures.

Creative language tasks, on the other hand, require learners to use whatever language they have at their disposal to complete the task. They are not restricted to following grammatical structures provided by the teacher or the textbook. I believe that such tasks facilitate language acquisition because they require learners to recombine familiar elements – phrases, lexical chunks, and so on – in new and unfamiliar ways. So the discourse in the classroom resembles more closely out-of-class language than does reproductive language work.

Scott Thornbury uses a nice analogy to capture this notion of grammar as a creative resource rather than as a product, that it's not just a thing but something you do. He says:

> An omelette is the product of a (relatively simple but skillful) process involving
> the beating and frying of eggs. The process and the product are clearly two

quite different things, and we could call one *making an omelette* (or even *omletting*) and the other an omelette. Similarly, the grammar that a linguist might identify in a statement like *If I'd know you were coming, I'd have baked a cake* or *Mary had a little lamb* is the result of a process – in this case an invisible mental one . . . To someone who had never seen an omelette being made, it might be difficult to infer the process from the product. They would be seriously mistaken if they thought that making an omelette was simply a case of taking a lot of little bits of omelette and sticking them together. So, too, with grammar. What you see and how it came to be that way are two quite different things.

(*Thornbury, 2001: 90*)

Question: Is it possible to get beginners using language creatively, in the way that you describe?

Response: Obviously, the less language that learners have, the more challenging it will be to implement creative language tasks. The more language that learners have, they more they have to work with, and the more successful the task is likely to be. However, I've found it possible to use creative tasks with even relatively low level learners.

TASK

Select a textbook and review the grammar exercises. These will not necessarily be explicitly labeled a 'grammar.' In one sense, all tasks and exercises should have a grammar dimension. Create an inventory of reproductive and another of creative grammar tasks.

Small Group Discussion

In this discussion thread, a group of students are discussing the role of consciousness in language acquisition as well as consciousness-raising tasks in the foreign language classroom. The discussion is a follow-up to a survey article that the students read prior to the discussion.

JAKE: So, what did you think of the article?

KIM: There was an awful lot to think about. I had to read it several times before I understood the arguments about conscious learning and subconscious acquisition. I find it hard to accept that there is a strict separation between conscious learning and subconscious acquisition.

SALLY: Why is that?

KIM: It just doesn't seem to make much sense. When we learn any skill – like learning to drive a car, for example, to begin with, we develop the skills consciously, but over the time they become automatic. We change gears, accelerate, brake, and do all of those other things without even thinking about it – the skills have become subconscious. If that's how learning occurs in learning how to drive and the other things we learn how to do, then why should language learning be any different?

JAKE: Well, language learning is a lot more complicated than learning to drive a car.

KIM: That's true, but I don't agree with the idea that we don't need to bother teaching grammar any more, that learners will 'pick it up,' if we just engage the learners in using the language. Also, my learners *expect* me to teach grammar. If I don't live up to their expectations, then I'll lose credibility. When I learned English in school, we spent most of our time doing grammar exercises of one kind or another, and I'm convinced that the grammar foundation gave me a solid basis for my language.

JAKE: Well how do you explain the fact that some learners *never* seem to acquire certain grammar items? My students know way more grammar rules than I do. They can tell me the rules, but half the time they don't use them. To me, this is pretty convincing evidence that conscious learning and subconscious acquisition are two different things. And most grammar rules are too complicated – you just get a feel for the way the language works by using it. Also, Kim, I have to tell you that when I lived in Italy, I didn't study the language formally. I just picked it up, and I was communicating quite well within a few months.

SALLY: I bet you had an Italian girlfriend, Jake.

JAKE: Well, I did as a matter of fact. How did you know?

TONY: I think the discussion only goes to show that learners are different and learn in different ways. Some learners like to just jump in there and pick the language up naturally; others like to study it more formally. Also, it's not the case that you either know a grammar rule or you don't. It's a gradual process. I liked the idea of consciousness-raising tasks, that gradually make the learners aware of the rule and how it works. Tasks and exercises raise their awareness of a grammatical principle but that doesn't mean they'll be able to use the principle or item immediately.

SALLY: What are some techniques for consciousness-raising? I'm still not clear about the concept.

TONY: Well, it could be traditional formal instruction, or it could be guided discovery – problem-solving tasks that draw the attention of the learners to the grammatical feature and how it works communicatively. Noticing a feature can also happen spontaneously through informal means such as error correction.

SALLY: Can you give an example?

TONY: Well, I saw a lesson once in which the teacher was teaching colors and clothing. She was getting the kids to prepare a fashion show. She brought in a big bag of clothes, and got the kids dressing up. Half the class dressed up and paraded up and down the classroom. The other half of the class had to be commentators. The grammatical focus was present progressive, where the kids were supposed to come up with statements such as "She's wearing a white shirt and a black hat," "He's wearing blue jeans and a yellow shirt." She found that the kids were using the present progressive accurately, but were putting the adjective after the noun, saying things like "the jeans blue" and "a hat black," because in their first language that's the way it's done. So the teacher just called the fashion parade to a halt for a minute – froze the action, as it were, and demonstrated the correct placement of the adjective *before* the noun. She got the students to practice saying "the blue jeans," "a black hat." So, that would be a good example of consciousness-raising through error correction, I'd say.

SALLY: Oh, I see. I get that example. Thanks.

Commentary

This discussion thread emphasizes that there are many different ways of raising learners' awareness about a particular grammatical feature, from formal instruction to relatively informal consciousness-raising tasks to incidental learning.

TASK

Summarize the arguments for and against the idea that conscious learning and subconscious acquisition are two separate processes, i.e. that learning does not 'turn into' acquisition. Where do you stand on the issue?

Summary

Content focus	Teaching grammar
Vignette	The grammar dictation technique
Issue in focus	Deductive versus inductive teaching
Key principles	1. Integrate both inductive and deductive approaches into the teaching of grammar.
	2. Use tasks that make clear the relationship between grammatical form and communicative function.
	3. Focus on the development of procedural rather than declarative knowledge.
	4. Encourage learners to use language creatively rather than reproductively.
What teachers want to know	Functional grammar; reproductive versus creative language use
Small group discussion	Conscious learning versus subconscious acquisition; consciousness-raising in the classroom

Further Reading

Thornbury, S. (2000) *How to Teach Grammar*. London: Pearson.

This book covers the theory and practice of teaching grammar in the communicative era in an accessible and interesting way.

References

Cohen, L. and L. Manion (2007) *Research Methods in Education*. 6th Edition. New York: Routledge.

Doughty, C. and J. Williams (eds.) (1998) *Focus on Form in Classroom Second Language Acquisition*. Cambridge: Cambridge University Press.

Krashen, S. (1981) *Second Language Acquisition and Second Language Learning*. Boston: Heinle/Thomson.

Krashen, S. (1982) *Principles and Practice in Second Language Acquisition*. Boston: Heinle/Thomson.

Mouly, G. (1978) *Educational Research: The Art and Science of Investigation*. Boston: Allyn & Bacon.

Nunan, D. (2005) *Grammar*. New York: McGraw-Hill.

Nunan, D. (2013) *What is This Thing Called Language*. 2nd Edition. London: Palgrave Macmillan.

Pennington, M. (1995) A situated process view of grammar. In M. Pennington (ed.) *New Ways in Teaching Grammar*. Alexandria, VA: TESOL.

Thornbury, S. (2000) *How to Teach Grammar*. London: Pearson.

Thornbury, S. (2001) *Uncovering Grammar*. Oxford: Macmillan.

10
DISCOURSE

Goals

At the end of this chapter you should be able to:

- discuss 'register,' along with its components 'field,' 'tenor,' and 'mode,' and provide an example of how it can be used in a classroom task
- differentiate between the four modes of classroom discourse
- describe three important principles for teaching discourse
- define exchange structure analysis and adjacency pairs

Introduction

In the three preceding chapters, we looked at ways of teaching the three linguistic subsystems of sounds, words, and grammar. In this chapter, we turn to discourse. Discourse is not a system, although it is systematic. I won't go into a great deal of detail in this chapter as to why discourse does not constitute a system. Basically, it lies in the fact that linguistic subsystems can be studied independently of the individuals and the contexts which produced them. They exist on the page or in the recording device. Discourse exists within the communicative context in which it was created, and can only be studied within that context. (For a detailed discussion on this issue, see Nunan, 2013b.) Elsewhere, I defined discourse as "any stretch of spoken or written language viewed within the communicative context in which it occurs" (Nunan, 2013a: 221). McCarthy and Walsh (2003) draw the following contrast between grammar and discourse:

> Grammarians study sentences, pieces of language taken out of context. The rules for using the English past tense, for example, can be stated generally

without reference to any particular context or situation. When we study discourse, however, we are interested in why someone chooses a past tense in a particular situation when addressing a particular listener . . . Important questions in the study of discourse are:

- What is the relationship between the speakers and how is this reflected in their language?
- What are the goals of the communication (e.g. to tell a story, to teach something, to buy something)?
- How do speakers manage topics and signal to one another their perception of the way the interaction is developing? How do they open and close conversations? How do they make sure they get a turn to speak?

(McCarthy and Walsh, 2003: 174)

These contextual factors have a major influence on the nature of the discourse that emerges. Causal conversations at a dinner party are different from the language of the law court, which is different again, from a medical consultation.

Most classroom discourse is different from discourse outside the classroom. Consider the following conversational fragment:

A: What's the date today?
B: It's September 30th.
A: It's September 30th. Very good.

There is something odd about the third utterance in the conversation. Normally, we would expect something like this:

A: What's the date today?
B: It's September 30th.
A: Thanks very much.

In fact, the first version is a piece of classroom discourse, where the point of the question from A (the teacher) is not to find out the date, but to get the student to display their knowledge of a particular grammatical structure: It + be + date. This is one of four basic discourse modes that occur in the classroom. (We will look in greater detail at this and the other classroom discourse modes in the 'issues in focus' section of the chapter.)

The example above illustrates a basic discourse pattern in classrooms of all kinds – not just language classrooms. This is known as the Initiation–Response–Follow-up, or IRF, pattern. The teacher initiates the interaction, usually through a question, a student responds, and the teacher follows up, usually through some form of evaluation of the student's response.

A fundamental question asked by grammarians is "What distinguishes a grammatical sentence from an ungrammatical sentence?" Why is sentence A, below, acceptable, while sentence B is nonsensical?

A: The dog bit the man.
B: The bit the dog man.

The answer can be found in the arrangement of the words on the page. Sentence A conforms to one of the syntactic rules of English – that a subject should be followed by a verb which, unless it is an intransitive verb, should be followed by another part of speech such as an object or a complement. The answer can be determined without reference to the creator of the sentences.

Discourse analysts ask a similar question. "What is it that distinguishes a random collection of utterances from a coherent collection of utterances?" Why does conversation A make more sense than conversation B?

Conversation A

A: What's the time?
B: It's eight o'clock.

Conversation B

A: What's the time?
B: The mouse ran up the clock.

Most people reply that A makes sense because the response answers the question. In B, there seems to be no connection between the question and the response, although, with a little ingenuity, we can probably create a context where the response makes sense.

A: What's the time?
B: (I can't tell you.) The mouse ran up the clock (and broke it).

The point here is that meaning resides, not on the page, but in the heads of the listeners, speakers, readers, and writers. We *make* sense, we don't simply discover it on the page. In a nutshell, this is why discourse, while it is systematic, does not constitute a system.

One more concept that you need to be familiar with is 'register,' an important concept within discourse analysis. Originally developed by the functional linguist, Michael Halliday, it is closely related to the preceding discussion on the importance of contextual factors to discourse. In Halliday's concept of register, the three most important contextual variables are, first, the topic of a communicative event (which he calls "field"), the relationship between the people taking part (which he calls "tenor") and the channel of communication: for example, whether it is spoken or written, a face-to-face conversation or a telephone conversation, an email or a written note, etc. (this is called "mode"). In the vignette that follows, we will see the teacher using this concept of register as the basis for a lesson.

Vignette

This lesson takes place in an advanced EFL speaking class. At the beginning of the lesson, the teacher reviews an earlier lesson in which she introduced the concept of register.

"OK, then," says the teacher, "Let's get started. Remember the other day when we looked at the concept of register? I said that register consisted of three contextual variables, and by studying these variables we can account for how conversations – or other spoken or written texts – vary, and why they vary. What were the three important register variables we looked at? Yes, Joseph."

"The topic of conversation," replies a male student.

"Yeah, the topic or subject of the conversation – what the speakers are on about. And the technical term for this is . . .?"

"Field."

"Field. Field. Good. What was the second variable?"

Another student says, "The relationship between the speakers."

"And what was that called?" asks the teacher.

"Um . . . I forgot."

"Tenor," says a student before the teacher can reply.

"Yes, tenor. Good Christina," says the teacher. And, the third variable?"

"The mode."

"The mode. And what does mode mean?"

"The means of communication," replies the student. "If it's spoken or written, face-to-face or over the phone or the Internet. That kind of thing."

The teacher turns and creates the following table on the board.

field	*what the conversation is about*
tenor	*who the speakers are*
mode	*how the speakers communicate*

"So," she says, "there's a little summary. Now I'm going to play you three conversations, and I want you to identify the topic, the relationship, and the mode in each of them. And I want you to complete the following table as well as making a note of the language that enables you to do the task."

The teacher gets the students into groups and gives each group a copy of the following table.

Conversation	Field	Tenor	Mode
1			
2			
3			

She then plays the audio of the following conversations.

Conversation 1:

A: You look worried. What's up?

B: I just don't know what to get Dad for his birthday?

A: Isn't there anything in the catalogue?

B: I can't really find anything.

A: What about these ties?

B: Well, this one's OK, but hasn't he got one like that?

A: Yes, he does, but that's OK.

B: Hmm, I just think that ties are a kind of boring gift to give someone for his birthday.

Conversation 2:

A: Barbara Walker.

B: Hi Mom, it's me.

A: Oh, hi, what's up?

B: Oh, I'm trying to get something for Dad for his birthday.

A: And . . .?

B: And, I just can't think of anything.

A: Did you look in that catalogue I lent you?

B: I did, but I couldn't see anything.

A: How about the ties?

B: Oh, I didn't see those.

A: Take a look. They're on page nine. The blue one with the striped pattern is nice.

B: Hmm. It's just that ties are a pretty boring gift.

Conversation 3

A: Hi Baby.

B: Hi Honey.

> A: What are you doing?
> B: I'm trying to find a gift for my Dad.
> A: Hmm, what do you get the guy who has everything?
> B: Mom wants me to get one of these.
> A: Ties? The only thing worse than ties as a gift are socks! They totally suck.
> B: Well you're not a tie wearer. And your socks all have holes in them. So it's socks that you'll be getting next birthday!
> A: I can hardly wait!
> B: So what do you think of this one?
> A: I guess it's the kind of thing your Dad would like.

When the students have finished, the teacher gets their attention and does a debriefing. She asks one of the students to summarize the discussion they had for conversation 1.

"The field is buying a tie," says the student.

"Yes, OK," says the teacher, "but maybe you can make it a little more general – say 'buying a birthday gift,' or just 'gift buying.' Notice how there's a lexical chain running through the conversation that clearly marks the field – 'get,' 'birthday,' 'find,' 'ties,' 'one,' 'ties,' 'gift,' 'birthday.' You could identify the field from those words without even hearing the whole conversation. And how about tenor?"

"Mother and daughter."

"How do you know?"

"She says 'Dad'."

"But don't you think that they could both be daughters?"

The student pauses to think and then says, "Yes. But the first speaker sounds more like a Mom."

The teacher laughs and says, "OK, but there's nothing in the language that actually indicates this. Anyway, you could make it a little more general for tenor – say 'family members.' And then for mode?"

"Spoken, obviously. And face-to-face."

"How do you know face-to-face?"

"They are looking in a gift catalogue and use words like 'these,' 'ones,' 'one.' So it must be face to face."

"Excellent."

The teacher then turns a second group about conversation 2.

The student says, "For the field, it is the same as conversation 1 – gift buying. For the tenor it is 'family members' – mother and daughter, and . . ."

"How do you know it's mother to daughter?" interrupts the teacher.

"Speaker B says 'Mom'."

"OK, good. And the mode?"

"Telephone. We think it's telephone. Yes, for sure."

"And how do you know?"

"The speaker says her name – Barbara Walker. And then Speaker B says who she is . . ."

"So she identified herself," says the teacher.

"Yes, and that is telephone conversation."

"And, also, there's another clue that it's a telephone not face-to-face. Unlike conversation 1, the Mom uses more precise language. She doesn't say 'how about these' but identifies the page in the catalogue where the daughter should look. So the field and tenor are identical to conversation 1, but the mode changes, and the discourse is different as a result. Now, how about conversation 3? Joseph?"

"Field is the same – 'gift buying.' Mode is face-to-face."

"How do you know?"

"Like for conversation 1, they use words like 'these' and 'this one'."

"And for tenor?"

"We think girlfriend/boyfriend."

"Because?"

"They call each other 'Baby' and 'Honey'."

"But they could be husband and wife, couldn't they?"

"Hmm." The student considers this option and then says, "Maybe, but I think it's more like girlfriend/boyfriend."

The teacher laughs. "So you think by the time they get around to getting married, they'll be over calling each other 'Baby' and 'Honey'."

The students laugh.

"So," says the teacher, "In this task, you can see how the variables of field, tenor, and mode are useful for understanding discourse, and how they are evident in the language itself."

REFLECT

What 3 things did you notice in the vignette? Write them down in note form.

1. _____

2. _____

3. _____

My Observations on the Vignette

1. The teacher introduces students to metalanguage, that is, technical linguistic terms such as register, field, tenor, mode. These provide the learners with tools that they can use to become their own discourse analysts. The subject matter of the lesson is thus language itself rather than, for example, gift buying.

2. There is evidence of uptake. Uptake occurs when the teacher corrects or reshapes a student's contribution, and this is subsequently taken up by that student and others in the class. In the course of the feedback session, the teacher reshapes the first student's contribution at a couple of points. When the student says that the field is "buying a tie," the teacher suggests that this be generalized to "gift buying." In terms of tenor, she suggests "family members" rather than "mother and daughter." The other students subsequently use these terms in their own reports to the class.

3. Learners are using the language creatively; they are not just regurgitating models provided by the teacher or the materials.

4. In the debriefing, although the learners are using the language creatively, it is still 'classroom' language. It is the teacher who calls the shots, determining who gets to say what, and when they get to speak. In the next section, we will look at modes of classroom discourse. This extract is what is called 'materials mode' rather than classroom context mode. (Read on, and you will see what I'm talking about!)

Issue in Focus: Modes of Classroom Discourse

In this section, I want to focus on modes of classroom discourse. What is interesting about discourse is that it can be the explicit content focus of a lesson, but it is also the medium through which all content matter, whether it be listening, grammar, vocabulary, and so on, is delivered.

In this section, I am drawing on the work of Walsh (2001), a discourse analyst and teacher educator, who has developed procedures through which teachers can identify the different kinds of discourse that occur in the classroom. Walsh makes the important point that it is vital for teachers to understand the nature of classroom discourse because for many learners, the classroom provides their main, if not their only, exposure to discourse.

Through his investigation of language classrooms, Walsh has identified four different modes of classroom discourse. These have different goals and content foci, which result in language with distinctive discourse feature. These four modes are as follows:

Managerial mode
Materials mode
Skills and systems mode
Classroom context mode

Managerial mode, as the name implies, occurs when the teacher is managing the 'business' of the lesson or lesson segment, for example spelling out the goals for the lesson, setting up group work, giving an out-of-class assignment, or one of the many other tasks required for the effective management of learning. This mode occurs most often at the beginning of a lesson or at transition points during a lesson. Not surprisingly, it usually takes the form of a monologue by the teacher, as is the case in the following extract, where the teacher is functioning in managerial mode:

> TEACHER: OK, now the approach we're gonna take here – there will be some traditional grammar in this, but what I'm going to try to give you is some analytical skills. Of how to analyze your own writing. Skills that you can take away from here and use them, OK? It's not just grammar we're looking at. What we're looking at is how do I make myself understood to somebody else. Right? And how can I work on this on my own all of the time?
>
> *(Nunan and Lamb, 1996: 62)*

In materials mode, teaching and learning are directed by tasks and activities in a textbook or other forms of material. For example they might be completing comprehension questions, gap-filling exercises, and so on. The typical pattern of interaction in materials mode is the IRF pattern described in the introduction.

In skills and strategies mode, the classroom focus is either on one of the three subsystems of language (pronunciation, vocabulary, or grammar), or on one of the four skills (listening, speaking, reading, or writing). The following extract is an example of a classroom operating in skills and strategies mode:

> [The students have been working on interviewing people about their lifestyle and health habits. They have just listened to a recorded interview, and the teacher is now focusing them on question formation.]
>
> TEACHER: What about smokes? What's the question you can ask for smokes?
> STUDENT: Are you smoke?
> TEACHER: Are you smoke? (pauses and models the correct grammatical form) Do you smoke, or does she smoke? Does she smoke? What question does the interviewer ask? The interviewer? What question does the interviewer ask? What's the question here?
> STUDENT: You smoke?
> TEACHER: You smoke? You smoke? That's not a proper question, is it really? Proper question is do you smoke? So he says, "You smoke?" We know it's a question because . . . why? You smoke?
> STUDENT: The tone.
> TEACHER: The tone . . . the . . . the . . .what did we call it before? You smoke? What do we call it?
> STUDENT: Intonation.
> TEACHER: Intonation. You know by his intonation – it's a question.
>
> *(Nunan and Lamb, 1996: 110)*

Here the teacher's goal is to get the students to form complete yes/no questions with do/does. The irony is that she uses a piece of authentic interview data between native speakers, but then points out that the interviewer is not using a 'proper' question form. Again, the basic discourse pattern is a series of IRF exchanges.

The final mode is classroom context mode. In this mode, the students get an opportunity for genuine, real-world type discourse. The IRF pattern is abandoned, and the teacher plays a less prominent role, having the same conversational status as the students. Here is an example of this mode:

> STUDENT 1: Ahh nah the one thing that happens when a person dies my mother used to work with old people and when they die . . . the last thing that went out was the hearing about the person
> TEACHER: aha
> STUDENT 1: so I mean even if you are unconscious or on drug or something I mean it's probably still perhaps can hear what's happened
> STUDENT 2: but it gets . . .
> STUDENTS: but it gets/there are
> STUDENT 1: I mean you have seen so many operation and so you can imagine and when you are hearing the sounds of what happens I think you can get a pretty clear picture of what's really going on there
> STUDENT 3: yeah.
>
> *(McCarthy and Walsh, 2003: 181–182)*

In this interaction, the students do virtually all of the talking. They provide the content of the conversation and manage the turn taking. This contrasts with the sample extracts in the preceding modes where the teacher does the initiating and follow-up, and the students only get to respond.

Key Principles

1. Help Learners Develop Discourse Skills Through Engaging in Authentic Discourse

As we saw in the preceding section, in most classroom interactions, learners have relatively few opportunities for authentic discourse in which they nominate topics, and are involved in speaker selection and change. Rather they are cast in a reactive role, their contributions sandwiched between teacher initiation and teacher feedback. As I pointed out in discussing the vignette, although the students were using the language creatively, they were still cast in a reactive mode, with the teacher setting the agenda. This is not unexpected in the feedback or debriefing phase of a lesson. However, even here, there are options. In the group discussion phase, rather than having each group analyze each conversation, each group could be asked to only analyze one conversation. In the debriefing phase, the group that had analyzed conversation 1 would provide the feedback to the class. The rest of the class would ask questions and the teacher would take a back seat. The second group would present the analysis of the second conversation, and the third group would provide the feedback on the third conversation.

With this principle, I am advocating the development of procedural skills. In the preceding chapter, I drew a distinction between declarative knowledge and procedural knowledge in the teaching of grammar. Declarative knowledge involves knowing that. Procedural knowledge involves knowing how. In the vignette, the teacher is working on the development of declarative knowledge of how the register variables of field, tenor, and mode function. This can be a useful first step. However the learners also need opportunities to develop discourse skills by using them productively in real conversations.

2. Keep in Mind that the Classroom Has its Own Discourse

This is one of the key principles in the model developed by McCarthy and Walsh (2003). They make the point that there are occasions in which it is appropriate to engage in 'teacher talk.' We have already looked at some aspects of teacher talk – for example, the fact that the great majority of teacher questions are what are called display questions, that is, questions to which teachers already know, or think they know, the answer. However, as McCarthy and Walsh point out, it is also important to create contexts in which learners have the opportunity to use language that is more natural and genuinely communicative. This relates to point 1, above. They need to have opportunities to:

Nominate topics
Make contributions to the conversation when *they* want to, not only when invited by someone else (and also have the option *not* to contribute)
Negotiate and co-construct meaning
Ask other students for their opinions and ideas

3. Teach Language Systems from the Perspective of Discourse

A constant theme of this book is the importance of teaching language in context. This is one of the mantras of communicative language teaching. With the grammar-translation and audiolingual methods, grammar is taught as isolated sentences. The approach, of course, is very different. In grammar-translation, the rules are taught explicitly. In audiolingualism, the rules are acquired implicitly through pattern practice drills. However, there are very few grammar items that are not affected by the linguistic and communicative context in which the item occurs. Think about the example I used in the preceding chapter when I discussed the issue of the passive voice. There I argued that we need to make explicit to the learners, not only *how* the passive is formed, but also *when* and *why* it is used.

How can we do this? The answer is to introduce the item in context. In the previous chapter, I made the point that in a traditional approach, the teacher would introduce the passive by presenting a set of active voice sentences, and demonstrate how to transform the sentences into the passive.

The dog bit the man. → *The man was bitten by the dog.*

Following the model, the students then complete exercises in which they transform active voice sentences into the passive. They learn how to form the passive, but not when and why to use it. However, if the item is introduced in the context of a piece of discourse, the use of the passive makes sense. For example, the students could be given an exercise such as the following:

A. Study these conversations.

1. A: *What did the dog do?*
   B: *The dog bit me.*
2. A: *What happened to you?*
   B: *I was bitten by the dog.*

B. Now, match these answers with the following questions.
   The police caught the thief.
   The thief was caught by the police.

1. A: What happened to the thief?
   B: ....
2. A: What did the police do?
   B: ....

The teacher could then follow up by pointing out that the focus of the question will determine what comes first in the answer. In conversation 1, the focus is 'the thief.' In the second conversation, the focus is 'the police.' Grammarians call this thematization. In 1, 'the thief' is thematized; in 2, 'the police' are thematized.

Although, in discussing this principle, I have confined the discussion to grammar, it also holds for teaching pronunciation and vocabulary.

What Teachers Want to Know

A concept relating to teaching discourse that teachers want to know more about is exchange structure analysis and the related concept of adjacency pairs. In this section, the teacher responds to their concerns and provide examples that they can use in their teaching.

Question: What is 'exchange structure analysis'?

Response: Exchange structure analysis was originally developed by two British linguists, John Sinclair and Malcolm Coulthard. They belonged to a group of linguistics who wanted to discover 'rules' underlying well-formed discourse. Their work is analogous to that carried out by sentence level grammarians who describe the rules underlying well-formed sentences. "What's the difference between a grammatical sentence and a random collection of words?" the grammarians want to know. The discourse analysts ask, "What's the difference between a coherent piece of discourse, such as a conversation and a random collection of utterances?" In a book I wrote years ago, I called this the 'super sentence' school of discourse analysis because these linguistics wanted to analyze discourse using a similar set of procedures as grammarians. More recently, I argued that this approach was doomed to failure because, while 'well-formedness' at the level of the sentence exists in language, 'well-formedness' at the level of discourse exists in the heads of speakers and hearers (Nunan, 2013a). Despite this, linguists have discovered some important principles and patterns underlying discourse.

Because casual conversation is extremely complex, initially linguists analyzed discourse in more formal contexts such as courtrooms, doctor–patient/dentist–patient interactions, and so on. Sinclair and Coulthard (1975) chose to analyze classroom discourse. Their unit of analysis was the lesson. This was the equivalent to the grammarian's sentence. The lesson consisted of instructional chunks called transactions, which, if we pursue the super sentence metaphor, would be phrases. At the next level down, we have exchanges (words), which are made up of moves (morphemes). The basic level of analysis, the exchange, was typically made up of three moves.

Question: Can you give an example?

Response: Sure. I touched on this issue in the introduction to the chapter where I used the following example:

A: What's the date today?
B: It's September 30th.
A: It's September 30th. Very good.

Here we have a typical classroom exchange made up of three moves. The exchange is initiated by the teacher, usually by asking a question. This is followed by a student response, which in turn, is followed by a teacher follow-up or evaluation of the student's contribution. The exchange structure is thus called an I-R-F (or E) sequence.

Question: How does the concept of adjacency pairs fit in here?

Response: Adjacency pairs also belong to the super sentence school of discourse analysis. However, in order to explain these, I need to back up a bit and explain another term – 'speech act.'

The term 'speech act' describes utterances from a functional point of view. It answers the question "What is the speaker doing?" rather than the question "What is the speaker saying?" According to the linguist John Searle, we do a number of basic things with language. We

- get people to do things
- commit ourselves to doing something
- make statements about the world
- we alter some state of affairs with our utterance
- we express an attitude about a state of affairs

The Initiate, Respond, Follow-up moves are examples of speech acts.

So, let's return to the question. An adjacency pair is a two-part exchange in which the first utterance, by the nature of the speech act being performed, will demand a particular speech act in return. A greeting demands a greeting in return, a question demands an answer – which can take the form of a refusal or at least an explanation or excuse. The following responses to the question "How much did that shirt cost?" are all coherent:

"Thirty dollars."
"I've forgotten."
"I don't know – it was a gift."

Responses such as the following would generally not be seen as coherent.

"It's a sunny day today."
"I had cheesecake."

Question: How can we, as teachers, use this in our teaching?

The basic insight here is that we need to show learners that every time we speak, we are also doing something with language. And this works in different ways in different languages. Learners need to recognize what speakers are doing when they say something, and they need to perform these speech acts themselves. In English, when we encounter a friend or acquaintance on the street and ask "How are you?" we are not inquiring about their health, we're greeting them. The appropriate response would be "I'm fine, how are you?" Similarly, at the beginning of the working week, "How was your weekend?" is a form of greeting. A brief response (such as "OK," "Fine," or "The weather was pretty miserable") is appropriate. A lengthy narrative about your skiing trip to the mountains is not. "See you later" is a farewell, not an invitation to meet for a drink. "What time?" would be an inappropriate response.

There are many ways in which this aspect of discourse can be explored in the classroom. With lower-proficiency learners it can be done through role-plays, matching exercises, selecting the best response from a series of options, etc. With more advanced learners, you can explore indirect speech acts. This is when the speaker doesn't respond directly, but indirectly, and the interlocutor has work to do to figure out what speech act is being performed. Consider the following utterance:

"That's a nice bottle of wine."

What is the speaker doing here? Is she complimenting the owner of the bottle, describing the shape of the bottle, and the label, or requesting a drink? If it's a request, then it's an indirect one, and the listener has work to do to decide how to respond.

Small Group Discussion

Developing skills as a discourse analyst has a number of benefits. As we have seen, teachers can use their knowledge to design teaching materials and learning tasks for students. However, it also provides them with a lens for looking at their own language in the classroom. In this discussion, a group of teachers in preparation are discussing classroom talk, with a particular focus on teacher talk. The teachers have been brainstorming some of the things that teachers do with language in the classroom.

JAKE: Based on the reading that we've been doing and our classroom observations, we have to brainstorm the sort of things teachers do with language in the classroom. I suppose that the first thing they do is teach.

KIERA: What does that mean?

TIM: I suppose that if you ask the person in the street they'd say that teaching is imparting information. I know something that you don't. I tell you, and now you know. So I've taught you.

JAKE: I think that's a pretty narrow definition of teaching, isn't it?

TIM: Of course it is. But I'm saying that it's what the average person probably thinks. I read an article about teacher talk, and it called this view the "good news" approach to instruction. "Hey, guess what guys? Did you know that if you make statements in third person declarative, you have to put an 's' on the end of the verb."

KIERA: Well, you can laugh about it, but it *is* one of the things that teachers do. And it is something that learners expect. When they ask for a grammar explanation, for example, that's what they want. But there are other ways of getting information across to learners.

TARA: Like?

KIERA: Like various forms of error correction and feedback. I was observing a lesson the other day, and the teacher did this in a kind of subtle way. When the students made a mistake, the teacher simply repeated what the student said, but using the correct grammar.

JAKE: The problem with that technique is that the learner mightn't notice the correction.

KIERA: I talked to the teacher about that in the debriefing after the lesson. Some of the students self-corrected, and some didn't. The teacher said that she was aware of that. When they self-correct, it's called 'uptake.' She said that students will notice when they're ready to. She thinks that a lot of formal error correction is a waste of time because students aren't ready for it.

TIM: Another thing that teachers do is ask questions. Who read that article on teacher questions?

JAKE: I did.

TIM: Can you give us a summary of the article?

JAKE: Sure. It discusses the basic classroom interaction pattern – the teacher asks a question, a student answers, and the teacher gives feedback. Teacher questions in this type of interaction are called display questions because the purpose is to get the students to display their knowledge or to show their mastery of some grammar point or vocabulary item. That's one thing that differentiates classroom talk from everyday talk. Outside of the classroom, if you go up to a stranger and ask "Is this a watch?" you might get into trouble, but in the classroom we do it all the time. The article says that in the classroom, teachers rarely ask genuine questions – ones that they don't know the answer to.

TARA: The article I read was all about that.

TIM: About what?

TARA: About the use of genuine questions in the classroom. They're called referential questions by the way. The researchers found that when teachers deliberately increased the number of referential questions in the classroom, the students' responses changed.

TIM: In what way?

TARA: Their answers became longer, and more complex, and the classroom discourse became more like discourse outside of the classroom. Often the teacher had to negotiate meaning to clarify what the student had said, other students contributed to the discussion and so on.

TIM: Well, it makes sense. If the teacher asks a question and doesn't know the answer, then it puts the learner in control of the classroom discourse – for a short time, anyway.

KIERA: Of course, questions aren't always used to obtain information. They're also used to control behavior. In that lesson I observed, at one point some of the kids were getting a bit unruly, and the teacher asked one of them if he was talking. She didn't really want to know the answer because she already knew. She wanted the kid to shut up and pay attention because she was about to set up a new task. So, questions can be used for classroom management and discipline.

Commentary

Teacher talk fulfills many functions: for classroom management, to provide information, to elicit student language, to correct learner language – the list goes on. In this discussion, the teachers in preparation focus on direct instruction, error correction and feedback, and teacher questions. They also discuss some of the features of classroom discourse that differentiate it from non-classroom discourse.

Summary

Content focus	Discourse
Vignette	Register as a tool for analyzing discourse
Issue in focus	Modes of classroom discourse: managerial, materials, skills and systems, and classroom context modes
Key principles	1. Help learners achieve discourse skills through discourse.
	2. Keep in mind that the classroom has its own discourse.
	3. Teach language systems from the perspective of discourse.
What teachers want to know	Exchange structure analysis; adjacency pairs
Small group discussion	Classroom discourse

Further Reading

McCarthy, M. and S. Walsh (2003) Discourse. In D. Nunan (ed.) *Practical English Language Teaching*. New York: McGraw-Hill.

This is an accessible introduction to classroom discourse. In it, McCarthy and Walsh introduce their mode of classroom discourse and discuss practical techniques for the classroom.

References

McCarthy, M. and S. Walsh (2003) Discourse. In D. Nunan (ed.) *Practical English Language Teaching*. New York: McGraw-Hill.

Nunan, D. (2013a) *What is This Thing Called Language?* 2nd Edition. London: Palgrave Macmillan.

Nunan, D. (2013b). *Learner-Centered English Language Education: The Selected Works of David Nunan*. Chapter 9: Discourse and language systems. New York: Routledge.

Nunan, D. and C. Lamb (1996) *The Self-Directed Teacher*. Cambridge: Cambridge University Press.

Searle, J. (1969) *Speech Acts: An Essay in the Philosophy of Language*. Cambridge: Cambridge University Press.

Sinclair, J. and M. Coulthard (1975) *Towards an Analysis of Discourse*. Oxford: Oxford University Press.

Walsh, S. (2001) Characterizing teacher talk in the second language classroom: A process approach of reflective practice. Unpublished Ph.D. thesis, Queen's University of Belfast, Northern Ireland.

11
LEARNING STYLES AND STRATEGIES

Goals

At the end of this chapter you should be able to:

- define learning styles and strategies, and state how they are related
- create at least three tasks for teaching strategies in the classroom
- describe three important principles for teaching learning strategies
- describe 3–5 ways in which 'good' language learners are different from not-so-good learners

Introduction

At several points in this book, I have argued for a twin focus in language learning and teaching. One focal point is language content, the other is learning processes. The former addresses the *what* of language teaching and learning; the latter focuses on the *how*. In this chapter, I will deal with issues to do with language learning processes.

A learning style is the natural, habitual way that we go about learning. Learning styles have been classified in various ways. Christison (2003), for example, distinguishes between cognitive styles, sensory styles, and personality styles. Cognitive styles include field dependence and field independence. Sensory styles distinguish between learners who prefer to learn visually, that is, by seeing language written down, as opposed to those who prefer to learn by hearing, or kinesthetic learners who learn best by physically manipulating objects in the environment.

Learning strategies are the cognitive and communicated processes that learners use in order to acquire a language. Common strategies include memorizing, repeating, inferencing, and predicting. In my 1999 book, I classified strategies into five broad categories: cognitive, interpersonal, linguistic, affective, and creative. These are reproduced in the following table.

Cognitive

Classifying
Putting things that are similar together in groups
Example: Study a list of names and classify them into male and female
Predicting
Predicting what is to come in the learning process
Example: Look at unit title and objectives and predict what will be learned
Inducing
Looking for patterns and regularities
Example: Study a conversation and discover the rule for forming the simple past tense of regular verbs
Taking Notes
Writing down the important information in a text in your own words
Concept Mapping
Showing the main ideas in a text in the form of a word map
Inferencing
Using what you know to learn something new
Discriminating
Distinguishing between the main idea and supporting information
Diagramming
Using information from a text to label a diagram

Interpersonal

Co-operating
Sharing ideas and learning with other students
Example: Work in small groups to read a text and complete a table
Role-Playing
Pretending to be someone else and using the language for the situation you are in
Example: You are a reporter. Use the information from a reading text to interview the writer

Linguistic

Conversational Patterns
Using expressions to start conversations and keep them going
Example: Match formulaic expressions to situations

Practicing
Doing controlled exercises to improve knowledge and skills
Using Context
Using the surrounding context to guess the meaning of unknown words, phrases, and concepts
Summarizing
Picking out and presenting the major points in a text in summary form
Selective Listening
Listening for key information without trying to understand every word
Example: Listen to a conversation and identify the number of speakers
Skimming
Reading quickly to get a general idea of a text
Example: Deciding if a text is a newspaper article, a letter, or an advertisement

Affective

Personalizing
Learners share their own opinions, feelings, and ideas about a subject
Example: Read a letter from a friend in need and give advice
Self-Evaluating
Thinking about how well you did on a learning task and rating yourself on a scale
Reflecting
Thinking about ways you learn best

Creative

Brainstorming
Thinking of as many new words and ideas as you can
Example: Work in a group and think of as many occupations as you can

(Adapted from Nunan, 1999: 183–184)

Vignette

In this vignette, the teacher is working with a group of international students from a range of countries in an EAP class which is preparing them for university entry. The teacher is highly experienced, and has focused her teaching on strategies for dealing with academic English. In this lesson, she is giving the students practice in using context to figure out the meaning of an unknown word. She begins by reminding the students of the importance of strategies. She begins the lesson by saying, "In this course, I've been teaching you strategies for effective learning as well as teaching you language. Why have I been focusing so much on strategies?"

"So we can learn on our own," replies one of the male students.

"That's right, Igor. At the beginning of the course, you thought it was a bit strange that we were focusing so much on strategies, but I pointed out that we only have a comparatively short time together and that the best use of this time was for me to teach you strategies so that you can go on learning when we're no longer together. See – I'm trying to do myself out of a job!"

The students laugh. "We don't want you be out of a job," says Igor.

"That's very kind, but I judge my success as a teacher on that. When you don't need me any more, I know I've succeeded as a teacher," says the teacher. "Anyway, this week, we've been looking at strategies for learning new words. Yesterday, we looked at how dictionaries can help, and at all of the useful information that you can get from a dictionary about an unknown word. Today, we're going to look at another strategy – using context to figure out the meaning of an unknown word. Why do you think that this is an important strategy? Heidi?"

"Because if we use dictionary, it will be too slow," replies one of the female students.

"Yes, if you use your dictionary to look up every word, then it will make the reading very slow. And there'll be circumstances when it isn't practical to use a dictionary. So, now we're going to look at how you can use context to find the meaning of a word. So, I have a passage here from a short story by the British writer Somerset Maugham. I picked it because it has some words that I'm pretty sure you don't know. You're all so good, that it was hard to find a passage with unknown words."

The students laugh at this. The teacher hands out the following text, and gives the students time to read the extract.

THE FORCE OF CIRCUMSTANCE

She was sitting on the verandah waiting for her husband to come in for luncheon. The Malay boy had <u>drawn</u> the <u>blinds</u> when the morning lost its freshness, but she had partly raised one of them so that she could look at the river. Under the <u>breathless</u> sun of midday, it had the white <u>pallor</u> of death. A native was <u>paddling</u> along in a <u>dug-out</u> so small that it hardly showed above the surface of the water. The colours of the day were <u>ashy</u> and <u>wan</u>. They were <u>but</u> the various <u>tones</u> of the heat.

"You'll notice that I've underlined some of the words in the passage," says the teacher, "and these are the ones I want you to discuss. Some of them I'm sure that you don't know – like 'pallor.' Others, like 'drawn,' you do know, but they have a meaning in the passage that you probably don't know. I want you to work in small groups to discuss the passage, and in particular the underlined words. But before you get into groups, let's take a look at the underlined words in the second sentence. What does 'draw,' 'drawn' mean? Mahesh?"

The designated student consults the student sitting on his right and then says, "To make a picture – something like that."

"That's the usual meaning of 'to draw' – to create a picture or diagram with a pen or pencil. But does that make sense? 'The Malay boy had drawn the blinds'?"

Several students shake their heads.

"So it must mean something else," says the teacher. "How about 'blind.' It means 'unable to see,' but in this context it must mean something else. Does anyone know another meaning for 'blind'?"

A student says rather hesitantly, "Is it like a kind of curtain?"

"Yes, thank you Van, and even if you don't know that meaning for blind, you can figure it out from the context because in the second half of the sentence, we learn that 'she,' the wife, partly raises the blind so that she can see the river. So we know that a blind is something that cuts out the view such as a kind of curtain or a verandah shade. The text tells us that the Malay boy, presumably a servant or helper, drew the blind, but she partly raised it, so 'draw' must mean . . .?"

"Lower," says Van.

"Exactly," replies the teacher. "In this context, to draw the blind means to close or lower it. And we can get the meaning from the context. The passage has plenty of linguistic clues – words that you *do* know, and you can use them to figure out the words that you don't. OK?"

The students nod.

"Now, I've been a bit long-winded here. That means, I've talked too much!"

The students laugh.

"But I wanted to take you through the process of how you can use what you do know to figure out, or make assumptions about, the meaning of words that you don't know. What you need to do is to practice that strategy so that you can apply it automatically when you don't know a word. When you can do this, then you have acquired a new skill. Now, please get into your groups and work on the other words that are underlined."

REFLECT

A. What 3 things did you notice in the vignette? Write them down in note form.

1. _____

2. _____

3. _____

B. Write down 3–5 questions you would like to ask the teacher about the lesson.

My Observations on the Vignette

1. The teacher is very much concerned with teaching strategies so that students can continue developing their language proficiency independently. At the beginning of the lesson she reminds the students of the goals of the course, and also the rationale. This is important because there can sometimes be learner resistance if the learners don't understand the rationale behind what the teacher is doing.

2. Although, at the end of the vignette, the lesson segues into small group work, the vignette is very teacher centered. There is a time and place for this teacher-fronted, direct instruction mode, even for teachers who are adherents to a student-centered philosophy. The teacher explains the strategy of learning new words by using context, and then models the procedures for the students before letting them apply the strategy in small groups.

3. At the end of the vignette, the teacher makes the point that when a learner has mastered a strategy and applies it automatically in learning and using language, for that learner, the strategy has become a skill.

Issue in Focus: The Relationship Between Learning Styles and Strategies

We have seen that learning styles are our natural, preferred way of going about learning. Styles are thus internal to the student. Strategies are the procedures that underpin particular learning tasks. In completing a task, students are engaged in both learning strategies and communication strategies. Once a person has mastered a strategy and can apply it effectively in learning and using language, it has become a skill.

Styles and strategies are related in that a given style will be associated with particular strategies. A kinesthetic learner will learn new vocabulary by, for example, manipulating flashcards. An auditory learner will prefer to learn new words by hearing them. Very often, it becomes difficult to draw a hard and fast distinction between 'style' and 'strategy.' For example, 'visual' learning is a style as it describes a person's preferred way of processing information. However, the style can't be seen directly, it can only be inferred through what individuals do – they read extensively, skim articles to get a general idea of what the articles are about, and scan for specific information. These are all strategies. So, in a sense, styles can only be inferred from strategies.

A classic investigation into the relationship between styles and strategies was carried out in Australia by a small team of researchers led by Ken Willing (1988, 1989). The team wanted to investigate possible correlations between style and strategy preferences and biographical variables such as ethnicity, first language background, and level of education. Over 500 learners from different backgrounds were interviewed and completed a questionnaire of learning strategy preferences.

The results showed interesting patterns of learning strategy preferences. For example, those who liked to learn by studying grammar also liked studying English books and reading the newspaper; those who liked the teacher to direct their learning also liked to have a textbook.

Four learning styles emerged from this work. The researchers gave them the following labels: 'concrete' learners, 'analytical' learners, 'communicative' learners, and 'authority-oriented' learners. While most learners exhibited characteristics of more than one style, for each learner, a particular style tended to dominate.

Learners with a 'concrete' style tended to like games, pictures, films, video, audio tapes, talking in pairs, and practicing English out of class. 'Analytical' learners liked studying grammar, studying English books and reading newspapers, studying alone, finding their own mistakes, and working on problems set by the teacher. Those learners with a 'communicative' style liked to learn by watching and listening to native English speakers, talking to friends in English and watching television in English, using English out of class in shops, on public transportation, etc., learning new words by hearing them, and learning by conversation. Finally, 'authority-oriented' learners preferred the teacher to explain everything, liked to have their own textbook, to write everything in a notebook, to study grammar, to learn by reading, and to learn new words by seeing them. Interestingly enough, there was no correlation between the biographical variables and learning preferences. The researchers concluded that:

> None of the learning differences as related to personal variables were of a magnitude to permit a blanket generalization about the learning preferences of a particular biographical sub-group. Thus any statement to the effect that "Chinese are X", or "South Americans prefer Y" or "Younger learners like Z", or "High-school graduates prefer Z" is certain to be inaccurate.
>
> *(Willing, 1988: 150)*

The researchers concluded that learning styles and strategy preferences had more to do with personality and cognitive style than first language, ethnicity, or level of education. They also argued that learning styles were highly resistant to change.

Key Principles

1. Encourage Learners to 'Stretch' Their Styles

This is a principle that Christison (2003) argues for. She points out that styles exist on a continuum. She says that "By thinking of learning styles on a continuum, I can see more clearly what styles students are using in the classroom and can get a clearer picture on how to get them to 'stretch their learning styles' – particularly for those learners at the extreme end of the continuum" (274).

This is a very important point and one that is underpinned by research showing that learners are not 100 percent one type or another (Wong and Nunan, 2011).

Think, for example, of the analytical/global learning styles. Analytical learners work more effectively alone and at their own pace. Global learners, on the other hand, work more effectively in groups. While learners will be partly analytical and partly global, one of these styles will be preferred over the other. The point Christison makes is that we should encourage learners whose instinct is to study alone to spend more time working in groups, and vice versa. The same can be said of auditory versus visual learners. It's not the case that auditory learners never learn by reading, nor that visual learners read to the exclusion of listening. By getting learners to 'stretch' their styles, trying out ways of learning that don't come naturally to them, we will help them to become more flexible and more effective learners.

This view is not accepted by everyone. Years ago, for example, Willing (1988) argued that our style is part of our cognitive and personality makeup, and therefore can't change. However, more recent evidence suggests that styles are not as impervious as we previously thought.

2. Do Not Privilege Any One Style Over Another

This is another principle that is somewhat controversial. The general consensus is that while styles differ, one is not necessarily superior to the other. In other words, learners who prefer to study alone will not necessarily be better learners than those who to prefer to learn by listening. According to this view, analytical learners should be given the opportunity to spend more time studying alone than in groups, but they should also be given the chance to work in groups.

As I said in the preceding section, there is a close relationship between 'style' and 'strategy,' that 'style' is an abstract concept, and that we can only make inferences about styles by looking at what people do, that is, through looking at the strategies they deploy in learning and using language. There is some evidence that learners who use certain strategies are more 'effective' than others. For many years, researchers and teachers have been interested in the 'good' language learner. In the early 1980s, Rubin and Thompson (1983) published an influential book called *How to Be a More Successful Language Learner*. This book was based on research the authors carried out in which they identified what good language learners did as they went about acquiring language. More recently, Wong and Nunan (2011) also found that there were discernible differences between the strategies used by more successful learners than less successful ones. We will look at this research in more detail in the next section.

3. Be Aware of the Relationship Between Learning Styles and Teaching Styles

This third principle addresses the relationship between learning styles and teaching styles. Although the principal focus in this chapter is learning styles, we should not ignore teaching styles. The reason is that if your style as a teacher is at odds with the learning styles of some of your students, then the effectiveness of your teaching may be limited. If you have a collaborative teaching style, then the way you run your classroom may not suit authority-oriented learners who want the teacher to tell them what to do. If your teaching style is authoritative, even authoritarian, then you may not be suited to students who value autonomous learning.

It's also worth knowing your own learning styles. Your teaching style will be conditioned by your learning style. If, as a language learner, you prefer to learn by listening rather than seeing, as a teacher, you will have a natural inclination to favor aural over visual learning tasks. It will also be conditioned by your own learning experiences. As a school student, you will have spent around 15,000 hours in the classroom. The number of hours you spend training as a teacher is minuscule compared to this amount. (Dan Lortie maintains that our experience as a school student is a form of apprenticeship – the "apprenticeship of observation," as he calls it [Lortie, 2002].)

In discussing the pedagogical implications of his groundbreaking research, Willing argues that classes should be constituted on the basis of learners' preferred learning styles rather on levels of proficiency, age, learning goals, or one of the other more traditional ways of grouping learners. He argues that learning style is more important for arranging effective instruction than other learner variables such as language proficiency. If this rather radical notion were followed, you could have beginners and advanced learners in the same class.

Attractive as this might at first seem, I find it problematic on both practical and pedagogical grounds. In practical terms, I can't think of a single institution that I have worked at over the years (and I've worked in many) where this would be a practical proposition. Apart from anything else, it would require extensive retraining of teachers and learners. Another practical concern I have is which category of style would one select? If you grouped learners according to sensory style, you would have a class of visual learners, a class of auditory learners, and so on. However, these classes would be disorganized in terms of cognitive style. The field dependent learners would be distributed across the classes as would the field independent learners. If the learners were organized in terms of cognitive style, they would be disorganized in terms of their sensory style.

At a practical level, I have already made the case for getting learners to 'stretch their style,' that is, to experiment with ways of learning that don't come naturally to them. While this would not be impossible in a group constituted exclusively of a particular style, it would be unnatural. Classes containing learners with different styles provide much richer teaching and learning opportunities. The learners who prefer to learn independently can provide models and even suggestions and advice to those who prefer to learn collaboratively, and vice versa.

Given the fact that you will have learners in your classroom with a range of learning styles, you should vary your teaching to accommodate this range of styles. In other words there should be something for everyone. However, it's important that learners be given an opportunity to reflect on their learning experiences, to be aware of what they are being asked to do and why, and to experiment with different ways of learning.

What Teachers Want to Know

In this section, the focus is on the notion of the 'good' language learner, and the question of whether good language learners have different styles and use different strategies from poor language learners.

Question: Some of my learners are better than others. I have extremely mixed-ability groups, and wonder how to deal with it. Is there any literature on the 'good' language learner?

Response: Logic tells us that some learners will be better than others. As individuals we all have different skills and abilities. That's true for sports, music, or anything else, so it's not surprising that it's also true for academic subjects. Some learners are gifted at mathematics, while others are hopeless at it. Some learners are better at language learning than others. But that doesn't mean we shouldn't try to help all learners be the best they can at language, while at the same time recognizing that not all of our learners will be outstanding language users. Whether you're a language teacher or a tennis coach, you should have this attitude.

Question: Do they approach learning differently from less effective learners? I mean, do the good learners actually do things differently from poor learners?

Response: I've done two studies looking at the question of what good learners do. They both involved getting learners to complete a learning strategy preference survey as well as taking part in an interview. The first study involved forty-four learners who developed bilingual competence in English and a number of other languages such as Japanese in a range of foreign language contexts in Southeast Asia. The most important factor seemed to be using language to communicate outside the classroom. The good learners also said that they were encouraged to use their second language in school for real communication. Affective factors were also important: motivation, liking the language, and a strong interest in the language were frequently mentioned.

Question: How do you know what influenced what? Did motivation result in good language learning, or did being a good learner lead to higher motivation?

Response: The answer is – we don't. We only know that there is an association between these factors, but we can't say anything about the direction of the influence. We know that positive motivation and being a good learner go hand in hand, but we don't know which is the cause and which is the effect. However, it doesn't mean that we shouldn't do everything we can to increase the motivation of our learners.

Question: You only looked at good language learners. How do you know that poor language learners don't also do these things and have these attitudes?

Response: This is a good question. Some years ago, I did a study with a colleague in Hong Kong. We compared the styles and strategy preferences of 'more effective' and 'less effective' learners. (This was determined by their scores on a comprehensive, standardized English proficiency test.) We used the Willing (1988, 1989) survey, which we put online to facilitate the data analysis. The dominant learning style for the more effective learners was 'communicative,' while the dominant style for less effective learners was 'authority-oriented.' The five most popular strategies of the effective learners were watching/listening to native speakers, learning new words by seeing them, watching TV/videos in English, having conversations in class, and learning many new words. For the less effective learners, the five most popular strategies were having the teacher correct mistakes, learning English words by seeing them, having the teacher help talk about interests, having a textbook, and learning new words by doing something.

There were also significant differences in the learners' attitudes. The effective learners liked English, enjoyed learning it, and spent up to fifteen hours a week practicing it outside of the classroom. The less effective learners didn't like English much, and spent less than an hour a week practicing it outside of the classroom.

Question: What are the practical implications of this research? Can we get less effective learners to use the same kinds of strategies that more effective learners use?

Response: I think that we can encourage them in some ways, but others are more difficult. Getting all learners to become learning-strategy oriented by making strategies explicit in the classroom and showing them how to apply these is helpful. We can stress the importance of practicing outside the classroom, but we can't actually force our learners to do this. Also, we can't coerce them into liking English, but making our classes more enjoyable and engaging hopefully will have a positive effect on their attitudes toward the language. The general conclusion from this and other studies is that attitudes toward language and learning, and an independent learning orientation, rather than specific strategy choices, were the key factors differentiating the effective from the less effective learners. In the study, the effective learners saw language as a tool for communication. The less effective learners saw it as just another subject on the curriculum.

TASK

The research shows that effective learners go about language learning in ways that are different from less effective learners. What do you see as the three most important strategies used by effective learners? Brainstorm ways in which less effective learners might be encouraged to adopt these strategies.

Small Group Discussion

In this session, a group of teachers discuss the relationship between affective issues in the classroom and learning strategies.

JEN: I'm the group leader for this week, and I want to get us started on the topic of affective issues in the classroom and how learning strategies can help deal with these. To be honest I'm a bit confused about the idea that there's a relationship. I'm not sure that I can see one myself.

MARIA: Well, maybe we need to broaden things a bit – talk about teaching strategies as well as learning strategies.

AISHA: That's a good idea. But let's start by thinking about affective factors. Anxiety is a big factor in my classroom.

MARIA: My big issue is boredom. I teach Spanish to teenagers, and they get bored really easily. The problem is that they had a semester of Spanish in elementary school, and weren't taught very well. They haven't mastered some of the basics. I have to reteach basic grammar, and they tell me they've already been taught that stuff. I have to tell them, "Well you might have been taught it, but you haven't learned it." I can see them going to sleep before my very eyes.

ALEX: Maria, it seems to me as though the problem with your kids is lack of motivation. Motivation is the biggest issue I have to deal with in the classroom, I have to say.

JEN: Me too.

MARIA: Well, let's focus on motivation, and think about the strategies that might help motivate learners.

ALEX: Fine by me.

AISHA: Me too.

MARIA: First, we need to get clear about what we mean by motivation.

JEN: In that reading we had by Gardner, he says that it's a combination of factors – effort, a desire the learn the language, and favorable attitudes toward the language.

MARIA: Someone else – I can't remember who it was – said it was the psychological factors determining the amount effort a learner is prepared to put into language learning.

ALEX: There's also different kinds of motivation when it comes to language learning. There's instrumental and integrative.

MARIA: Oh, yes. What was the difference between them?

ALEX: Instrumental is when you're motivated to learn something because it will get you better grades in school or a better job with a higher salary or whatever, and integrative motivation is about wanting to learn something for its own sake – maybe identify with the culture or community that speaks the language.

AISHA: Maybe it doesn't have to be one type or the other in all cases. In some cases it could be a combination of the two types of motivation.

JEN: Well, for the purposes of our discussion, let's try and think of some of the reasons why our learners' motivation falls off, and that might suggest some strategies for overcoming lack of motivation. In my case, I know my learners get confused about what they're supposed to be doing and why. I taught a listening lesson the other day, and at the end of the class I did an informal survey. I asked the kids what the lesson was all about. One of them said it was a vocabulary lesson. I was amazed.

MARIA: So, in that case, the strategy would be to make the goals of the lesson clear to the learners. Spell them out at the beginning. I know that's a weakness in my own teaching. I know what I want the learners to achieve, but I don't spell it out to the learners. I just assume they'll know. But all too often, they don't.

AISHA: I guess that's partly true in the case of my learners, too, but I think there's a bigger issue for them.

MARIA: What's that?

AISHA: Well, I teach upper-intermediate learners, and they've reached that plateau where they can't see any results for their efforts. One student said to me the other day, "I spend all this time on English, but I just don't seem to be getting anywhere."

JEN: Well, I guess one learning strategy to deal with this problem is to get learners to be more reflective.

AISHA: In what way?

JEN: Well, get them to look back on a lesson or a unit of work, and have them identify what they've actually achieved. I have students keep vocabulary logs. At the end of a unit of work, I get them to write down ten new words that they've learned. They won't all write down the same words, but that doesn't matter, in fact it's a good thing. Over time, they can see that their efforts *are* paying off.

ALEX: Another idea would be to relate this to the strategy of making goals explicit. So at the beginning of a unit of work you might tell them that the goals for the week are, for example, to talk about what people are doing and to start a telephone conversation. At the end of the week, you could get them to complete a little survey. "This week, the goal was to talk about what people are doing. How did you do? Yes, I can do this. No, I need more practice." They become more reflective learners and they build up a record of achievement – just like Jen's vocabulary log idea.

MARIA: Another strategy that can help with motivation is co-operating – working together in small groups. My kids love working co-operatively. And they get really motivated if I get different groups competing with each other. I never have individual kids compete with each other – that can be really destructive for the kid who loses, but group competitions are fun.

Commentary

In this thread, the participants begin by discussing affective issues in general and then focus on the key issue of motivation. They brainstorm various strategies for enhancing motivation including setting clear goals, developing a reflective attitude toward learning, keeping records of achievement such as vocabulary logs, self-evaluation, and co-operative learning.

TASK

In this session, the teachers are discussing two factors that demotivate their learners: not knowing what they're expected to learn and not being able to see progress for their efforts. They then brainstormed possible strategies for dealing with these factors.

Reflect on your own experience as a teacher or learner. (It can be teaching or learning anything, not just language.) List some of the things you or your learners found demotivating. For example "I couldn't relate to the content of the lesson." "The material was too easy (or too difficult)." Then come up with possible teaching or learning strategies for dealing with these demotivating factors.

Summary

Content focus	Learning styles and strategies
Vignette	Using context to acquire new vocabulary
Issue in focus	The relationship between styles and strategies
Key principles	1. Encourage learners to 'stretch' their styles. 2. Do not privilege any one style over another. 3. Be aware of the relationship between learning styles and teaching styles.
What teachers want to know	Learning styles and strategies of the 'good' language learner
Small group discussion	Strategies for improving motivation and other affective aspects of the learning process

Further Reading

Nunan, D. (2002) Learning strategy training in the classroom: An action research study. In J.C. Richards and W. Renandya (eds.) *Methodology in Language Teaching*. Cambridge: Cambridge University Press.

In this study, I investigated the effect of strategy training on learners' attitudes to and awareness of their own learning processes. I have recommended it here because the study includes many examples of the learner training tasks I used with the learners in the study, and these are easy to replicate in a wide range of situations.

References

Christison, M.A. (2003) Learning styles and strategies. In D. Nunan (ed.) *Practical English Language Teaching*. New York: McGraw-Hill.

Lortie, D. (2002) *Schoolteacher: A Sociological Investigation*. Updated Edition. Chicago: University of Chicago Press.

Nunan, D. (1999) *Second Language Teaching and Learning*. Boston: Heinle & Heinle.

Rubin, J. and I. Thompson (1983) *How to Be a More Successful Language Learner*. New York: Heinle & Heinle.

Willing, K. (1988) *Learning Strategies in Adult Migrant Education*. Adelaide: National Curriculum Resource Centre.

Willing, K. (1989) *Teaching How to Learn: Learning Strategies in ESL*. Sydney: National Centre for English Language Teaching and Research.

Wong, L. and D. Nunan (2011) The learning styles and strategies of effective language learners. *System*, 39, 144–163.

12
ASSESSMENT

Goals

At the end of this chapter you should be able to:

- define assessment and evaluation
- differentiate between assessment of learning and assessment for learning
- state the main purposes for assessment, and when, in the instructional cycle, they will occur
- identify who should be involved in assessment
- describe five important principles for incorporating assessment into your teaching
- discuss the advantages and disadvantages of direct and indirect assessment
- demonstrate understanding of the relative merits of reliability and validity in the assessment process
- differentiate between formative and summative assessment

Introduction

This final chapter deals with assessment, although I also touch on evaluation because it is a closely related aspect of the curriculum. I also need to discuss it briefly because in some (mainly North American) contexts, evaluation is some-times used as a blanket term to cover both assessment and evaluation. I have privi-leged assessment because the main focus of what teachers do in their day-to-day work is assessment rather than evaluation.

Books on curriculum and methodology conventionally deal with assessment and evaluation in the final chapter. I have followed this convention, although I had some hesitation in doing so as, symbolically at least, it gives the impression that assessment and evaluation are the last activities to be carried out in the teaching/learning process. While it is true that we assess our students and evaluate our programs at the end of the course (this is known as summative assessment and evaluation), we also carry out assessment and evaluation tasks during a course. This is known as formative assessment and evaluation.

So, what do these two terms mean? How are they similar, and how do they differ? Evaluation is the 'bigger' concept. It consists of a set of procedures aimed at helping us answer the question "How well did the course (and how well did the teacher) do in meeting the needs of the students?" The focus of assessment is directly on the students and deals with the question "How well did the students do?" As I have said, both assessment and evaluation can take place at any time, and can be ranged on a continuum from formal to informal. When preparing a course, we may need to select a new course book. We obtain inspection copies of several potential books from the publishers and review them to identify the most suitable one. This is a form of evaluation. We might design a needs assessment survey and get colleagues to review it and provide feedback. This is also a form of evaluation. It's the same with assessment. From the first day of class, we will be assessing our students. We might set them a small group task, and make a note of any errors they make as they complete the task. This is an informal type of assessment.

At various points in the course, and again at the end, you might administer more formal assessments, either in the form of a test or through some other means. Students will do well on some of the items, indicating that they have achieved certain course goals, but not so well on others. In order to improve their performance, you need to know why they did well on some items but not so well on others. To find out why, you need to collect information other than the students' scores. Was it that the textbook was inappropriate? Was there something wrong with the teaching? Were there problems with the online component of the course? Was student motivation a factor? What kind of data will enable you to answer these questions? Where, how, and when will you collect these data? These are all evaluation questions, and they reveal the relationship between assessment and evaluation.

An important distinction to bear in mind is between assessment *of* learning and assessment *for* learning (Carless *et al.*, 2006). Assessment of learning provides information for external parties: the parents, the teachers, the institution, external funding authorities, and so on. Assessment for learning provides information for learners and teachers who can use the information to improve student performance. In other words, the assessment becomes a learning tool rather than a tool for judging the student.

Any teaching task can be an assessment task with the addition of criteria and feedback. Criteria are the statements that indicate how well the learner has to do in order to be deemed to be successful on a task. Criteria can be adjusted according to the level of the student and can relate to accuracy, fluency, or both. For example, on a listening task, the criterion might be how much information the learner is expected to extract.

"You are going to hear a person on the telephone describing themselves to the driver of a car pick-up service. She says six things about her appearance. Identify at least four of the statements, and then pick the person out in this scene of people on the street."

Feedback refers to the information that is provided on how well the learner has done. A key question here is to whom will the feedback be provided? Feedback to the student will take a different form from feedback to a director of studies or a panel chair. Will the feedback be quantitative (*"You scored 85 out of 100 on the vocabulary quiz"*) or qualitative (*"I thought you were all a bit hesitant in your oral presentations, so we need to work on your fluency next week. Doing additional shadowing exercises will help with fluency"*).

The key questions that we need to look at in considering assessment are:

What is the purpose of the assessment?
When will the assessment be carried out?
How will it be carried out?
Who will do the assessing?
How will the assessment outcomes be reported?
Who will be the recipient of the outcomes? (Brindley, 2003)

These are some of the questions that we will look at in the rest of the chapter.

Vignette

In this vignette, the teacher involves the learners in the assessment process. The class consists of a group of university level second language students who are learning oral presentation skills to prepare them for the requirements of several of their content courses where giving oral presentations is one of the formal assignments that they have to carry out for their final grade. The students have already prepared and rehearsed an oral presentation, which they will upload onto the course Moodle.

"OK," says the teacher, "so now that you've prepared and posted your presentations to the course website, the next step is for you to do a self- and peer-assessment of the presentation. This will be the final step before you then revise your presentation, and repost it to the site. That will be the presentation the examiners will assess for your final grade. Any questions?"

"So we have to assess ourselves? Why we can't get you to assess us?"

"Because I want *you* to develop skills in evaluating, criticizing, and improving your own language performance. I'm not going to be around forever you know!"

This last comment is delivered in a jovial tone of voice and the class laughs.

"So what I'm going to do is to show you a video of three oral presentations. These are by students who took this course a couple of years ago, so you won't know them. I should tell you that I have their written permission to show these videos. I'm going to call them Mary, Jack, and Jill. These are not their real names of course. I've given them English names to further protect their identity. After you've watched the videos, I want you to do two things, and I want you to do them in groups. First, I want you to rank order the presentations from best to worst. I don't think you'll have too much trouble doing this because I've selected presentations that are different in quality, and it shouldn't be too hard for you to pick the best from the worst. The next step is more difficult. I want you to then say *why* one presentation was excellent, one average, and one not so good. Got that?"

The students murmur their assent.

"Good. OK, I suggest that you get into your groups now. But make your own notes individually before you pool your ideas."

The students arrange themselves into groups of four or five and the teacher shows the three oral presentations, each of which takes approximately five minutes. She then gives the students time to share their individual ideas and come up with a joint response.

"OK, then," says the teacher after ten minutes. "I think that you've all had enough time to rank order the presentations and evaluate each speaker. Martina, could you tell the class who your group thought gave the best presentation?"

"Oh, Jill, for sure. Yes, Jill," says Martina.

"Yes, Jill," says another group.

"You all agree?" asks the teacher. The rest of the class nods.

"And what were the things that you liked about the presentation?"

Martine consults her notes and says, "Very clear. Step-by-step. Very easy to follow the argument. Nice pace – not too fast, not too slow. Great PowerPoint. She spoke confident."

"Confidently," interrupts the teacher.

"Confidently," repeats Martina. "She spoke confidently. She know what she talking about. We wish we could talk like that."

"Well, that's what you have to aim for," says the teacher. The class laughs. "That's the point of this exercise. Now, Stefan's group. Out of the two remaining presentations – Mary and Jack – which did you think was better?"

"This not so easy," says Stefan, "But we think Jack." Unbidden, Stefan then lists features that, in his group's opinion, ranked Jack second. There is general agreement around the class.

"All right, there seems to be general consensus that Mary gave the weakest presentation. Silvia, would you like to tell us what Mary did wrong?"

"Well, she was not very fluent. Even if she read her notes, she not very fluent . . ."

"Even *though* she read from notes, she wasn't very fluent," corrects the teacher. "OK, and . . .?"

"No eye contact," says one of the other students in Silvia's group.

"Yes, no eye contact," confirms Silvia. She consults her notes. "An no clear argument. Very confusing. She seem very confuse."

"Yes," said the teacher. "Notice how the things that Jill did well were the things that Mary didn't do so well, so we can use that to begin to develop our checklist of criteria for assessing an oral performance. 'Speaks confidently' would be one of these, and we could rate a speaker on a scale of 0 to 5 on that criteria. And that's your next task. I want you to get back into your small groups and create a checklist for assessing oral presentations. Here's a model that you can refer to. I don't want you to simply copy these criteria, because this checklist was created for a different purpose – to evaluate small group discussions. But you can follow the format as a guide. Remember, the checklist you come up with is the one that will be used, first as a guide for you to do a peer- and self-assessment of your own presentation. So you know what to look for to improve your presentation. And then it will be used by the two teachers who will be assessing you. So you will be assessed on your own criteria, not someone else's. OK, off you go."

Working in their small groups, the students create their own checklists. When they have finished, the teacher briefly leaves the room and makes copies of each checklist. She returns to the classroom and distributes these around the room so that each group has a copy of the other groups' checklists. Working together as a whole class, they then create a composite checklist from their group efforts. The teacher, acting as a moderator and scribe, creates the final version on her computer and prints it off.

"A good morning's work," says the teacher. "Time for a break." "After the break, I want you to pair up and go to the multi-media learning center. I want you to watch your partner's presentation and give feedback based on the checklist that we've just created. Then you'll have three days to revise and improve your presentation. The final presentation needs to be posted to the website by Friday. Good luck, and I'll see you tomorrow."

REFLECT

A. What 3 things did you notice in the vignette? Write them down in note form.

1. _____

2. _____

3. _____

B. Write down 3–5 questions you would like to ask the teacher about the lesson.

My Observations on the Vignette

1. The aim of the exercise is self-assessment. Rather than being given a set of criteria for judging performance, the learners generate their own criteria inductively by analyzing the performance of others.
2. The activity illustrates the notion of assessment for learning. The aim of the exercise is assessment for learning rather than assessment of learning, as the intention is to improve performance, not to give a score or rating.
3. Peer assessment is part of the activity. Very often learners do not like being evaluated by their peers, but this exercise is structured in such a way as to make it non-threatening, supportive, and collaborative. The opportunity to be assessed by another student, and, in turn, to assess that other student, refines students' critical faculties.

Issue in Focus: Purposes for Assessment

In the introduction to this chapter, I listed the key questions that need to be considered in making decisions about assessment. In this section, I will look at the crucial issue of the purposes for and timing of assessment. There are two questions here: why do we assess and when do we assess? It's important to keep in mind that all of these questions are interrelated. For example, deciding who is going to be involved in the assessment, how the learners will be assessed, how the results will be reported, and who is the intended audience for the results of assessment, are also implicated in the questions of why and how.

There are many purposes for assessment. These are the ones I want to discuss here:

-   To place students in learning groups (we tend to think of these as classes, or other types of face-to-face learning groups, but there are also other ways of grouping learners, particularly in online and out-of-class learning).
-   To provide feedback on learners' strengths and weaknesses for course planning purposes.
-   To provide feedback on progress.
-   To provide evidence of the achievement of course goals.
-   To encourage learners to take responsibility for their own learning.
-   To provide records of achievement.
-   To provide information for accountability purposes.

Grouping students for learning is the first purpose that we will look at. In terms of timing, this assessment is carried out before instruction begins and normally it takes the form of some kind of proficiency test. This is because the principal criterion for grouping learners in most institutions is their current language ability. In elementary and secondary school, learners are first grouped according to chronological age. They are then further grouped. A philosophical issue that needs to be addressed at this point is whether the students are subgrouped according to ability, or whether the institution will have mixed-ability grouping. While mixed-ability groups present challenges for the teacher, they are more socially equitable as they do not stigmatize lower-proficiency learners. Looked at purely from a pedagogical point of view, however, it could be argued that grouping learners according to proficiency and ability enables teachers to tailor their instruction more closely to their instructional needs, for example, of gifted learners on one hand, and less talented language learners on the other. Given the fact that not all learners progress at the same rate, another factor that needs to be taken into consideration is whether to assess and reassign students to different learning groups during the course of a semester.

The assessment of learners' strengths and weaknesses is closely related to placement for course planning purposes. This is another purpose that is carried out prior to the beginning of instruction, although it will also be carried out, usually somewhat informally, during the course of instruction as the teacher monitors students to identify what is going well and what is not. This is known as diagnostic assessment and can be part of an initial proficiency assessment for placement purposes. When selecting a diagnostic assessment tool you need to decide exactly what aspects of learner language you wish to diagnose, for example, the four skills (listening, speaking, reading, writing), the language systems (pronunciation, vocabulary, and grammar), or functional aspects of language use.

In the introduction to the chapter, I talked about the distinction between assessment for learning and assessment of learning. Assessing learners and then providing them with feedback on where they are succeeding as well as indicating areas where further work is needed illustrates the notion of assessment for learning. The assessment is not carried out for final certification but to provide learners with a 'snapshot' of what they are doing well and where they need to improve. This assessment can be carried out informally, through observation and feedback, or it can be done more formally.

Providing evidence of the achievement of course goals is a fundamental purpose of assessment. This can be done formatively, during a course, or summatively, at the end of a course. When done formatively so that the results can be fed back to the learners, it exhibits instruction for learning. Alternatively, it can be done at the end of a course. This summative assessment exemplifies assessment of learning. It is an essential step in the evaluation process. Having decided which objectives have been achieved and which have not, the next step is to decide what adjustments need to be made the next time the course is run.

Encouraging learners to take responsibility for their own learning is another example of assessment for learning. In the vignette, we saw an example of a teacher encouraging learners to take responsibility for their own learning by training them to identify and employ performance criteria in their oral presentations. There are many forms of self-assessment. These may be very informal, such as at the end of a task, when you ask students "How do you think you went on the decision-making task we did today? Perfect? Not bad? So-so? Could do better? If you did the task again, what would you do differently? How would you like to improve?"

More formally, self-assessment checklists of one kind or another can be used. For examples of these checklists, take a look at the chapter on assessment in my book on task-based language teaching (Nunan, 2004).

Summative assessment is carried out for two main purposes: to provide learners with records of achievement, and to provide evidence of the effectiveness of instruction to other stakeholders such as parents, institutional managers, funding authorities, and so on. One of the dangers in many educational contexts where the stakes are high (for example, where the assessment will determine whether a student gets into university or not), is that doing well on the test dominates students' learning efforts. This sometimes leads to a situation where teachers teach, not to the course goals and objectives, but to the final test, and courses become an extended test-preparation exercise.

Somebody pays for the courses we teach. It could be parents, a government agency, or the management group of a private school or institution. Institutional management also wants to know if we are doing our jobs effectively. When assessment data are used to provide evidence of value for money or for efficiency, they are being used for accountability purposes. This is a purpose that sometimes makes teachers uneasy, but is essential for the long-term health, and, in some cases, the survival of an institution.

Key Principles

1. When Designing Assessments, Always Begin with the Objectives of the Course

Referencing assessment against the objectives of the course should be the major criterion for the assessment exercise. The objectives provide the overall rationale for the course. The assessment should tell you how well the students have done. This kind of assessment data will also be needed when it comes to evaluating the courses – deciding what objectives have been fully achieved, which only partially achieved, and which not at all achieved.

2. Involve Learners in the Learning Process

When deciding who should be involved in assessment, the learners are often overlooked. It is sometimes questioned whether learners are in a position to make judgments on their own performance. With the kind of carefully scaffolded learning such as is illustrated in the vignette, we can see that this is entirely possible.

3. Ensure that the Assessment Tool Is Appropriate to the Purpose of the Assessment

An assessment instrument can sometimes serve more than one purpose, but this is not always the case, so think carefully about why you are assessing learners when selecting the means of assessing them. A summative proficiency assessment will not necessarily be the right tool for identifying student strengths and weaknesses. A self-assessment exercise will not, on its own, be suitable as a record of achievement.

4. Do Not Use Assessments that Have Been Carried Out for One Purpose for Other Purposes

This is closely related to the preceding purpose. I once witnessed a situation in which assessment data that had been gathered as part of a diagnostic procedure to identify learners' weaknesses were subsequently used summatively by the school administration to make judgments on the program. Needless to say the judgments were quite negative, and unfairly so.

5. The Ultimate Judge of Success Is the Interlocutor Beyond the Classroom

The crucial test of a learner's language is whether other people can understand it in genuine communication outside the classroom. I remember once, as a very young teacher, being castigated by my learners. I had been heaping praise on their performance in an effort to boost their confidence, when one said to me. "You say our English is great, but when I try to use my English outside the classroom, people say they can't understand me."

What Teachers Want to Know

The point of departure for this discussion is the distinction between direct and indirect assessment, and the advantages as well as the disadvantages of both types of assessment.

Question: What's the difference between direct and indirect assessment?

Response: First, let's deal with indirect assessment. It's called 'indirect' because the assessment itself doesn't resemble the kind of things that we do with language outside the classroom. So we administer some kind of assessment, and then have to make inferences about what the learner can do as a result of the performance on the assessment.

Question: Can you give an example?

Response: Consider the following exercise.

Underline the correct word in parentheses.
Example: You have a headache. You (<u>should</u>/shouldn't) go to bed.

1. He's hungry. He (should/shouldn't) eat something.
2. They're very tired. They (should/shouldn't) do strenuous exercise.
3. You're stressed out. You (should/shouldn't) stay home and relax.
4. He's exhausted. He (should/shouldn't) keep working out.
5. I'm putting on weight. I (should/shouldn't) eat junk food.

On the surface, you might say, that if someone underlines the correct word that they have mastered the function of 'giving advice.' However, this is not really accurate. The best we can say is that the person can manipulate the modal verb should/ shouldn't. We then make an inference that, on the basis of their ability to complete the exercise successfully, they can give advice. This may or may not be borne out in actuality.

Question: So in a direct assessment, is there a direct relationship between the assessment and what we have to do outside the classroom?

Response: Yes, there is. Thus the label 'direct.' It's important to bear in mind that the indirect–direct distinction is a continuum. Anything we do in the classroom will be indirect to a degree. A more direct way of assessing the ability to give advice would be to create a small group simulation in which one member of the group has a problem, which the other members of the group have to help solve. This comes much closer to the real world than the indirect 'underline the correct word' example because the learners aren't given the language to manipulate; they have to generate it themselves. Just as important, they will use a range of other language functions such as making suggestions, agreeing, disagreeing, and so on.

Question: I understand the distinction now, so my question is, why do we have indirect assessments if they don't really tell us much about how learners can use language in the real world?

Response: That's a good question. The answer is that indirect assessment items are reliable and objective.

Question: What does that mean?

Response: Reliability has to do with consistency. It doesn't matter who marks the student responses, the result will be the same. In this example, they either underline the correct word or they don't. Also if you get the students to do the assessment task a second time – say the following week – you'll get the same response. The more direct the assessment, the greater the difficulty we have with reliability. Think about the small group simulation. How do we go about assessing the students? We could have a checklist that includes things like 'negotiates meaning effectively,' but this is a relative matter. Two different raters may interpret a given student's participation on the simulation differently. One rater may think that a given learner is effective in bringing in other speakers. Another rater may disagree. One rater may give greater weighting to accuracy of pronunciation, while another rater may give a higher weighting to fluency. Again, if we repeat the assessment the following week, a student's performance may be affected because he or she isn't feeling well.

Question: So, if the advantage of indirect assessment is reliability or consistency, what's the advantage of a direct assessment?

Response: Well, as I said, it gives us a better indication that the learner can perform the functions we're looking for in the world outside the classroom. So we're applying a different criterion measure. Rather than reliability, our criterion is validity. Validity has to do with whether the item is assessing what we are trying to teach – which is communicative ability in the world outside the classroom.

Question: I teach young learners. Do you have any suggestions for how I can assess the younger age groups?

Response: Many of the techniques used with older learners can be adapted for younger learners. I would certainly adopt the assessment *for* learning rather than the assessment *of* learning approach with younger learners. The assessments should be part of the teaching process. Informal observation can often be as effective as more formal means. An excellent resource, with many good ideas for assessing younger learners, is Ioannou-Georgiou and Pavlou's (2003) book on assessing young learners.

TASK

Examine a number of assessment items in a course book, or test package, and evaluate them in terms of their reliability and/or validity.

Small Group Discussion

In this discussion thread, a group of TESOL teachers are reporting back to each other on a technique for assessment that they have investigated and used in their classroom.

JUDY: I decided to look at observation and recycling of work. I decided on this assessment technique because we're always using informal observation and monitoring to make judgments about what learners are doing well, and where they need to improve. However, I decided to make the process a bit more systematic. One of the goals of my course is to improve my students' group discussion skills, which is something they're weak in.

VAN: How did you do that?

JUDY: I came across a whole lot of observation tasks and checklists in Ruth Wajnryb's (1992) book on classroom observation, and used one of the tasks in that book, with a few modifications.

VAN: Can you share one of the checklists with us?

JUDY: Sure. (She posts the following checklist to the group.)

Indicate the degree to which learners contribute to small group discussion by circling the appropriate number.

STUDENT NAME: _____

1 – excellent
2 – very good
3 – not bad
4 – needs more work

The student participates in discussions. (1 / 2 / 3 / 4 / 5)
The student uses appropriate non-verbal signals (1 / 2 / 3 / 4 / 5)
The student's contributions are relevant (1 / 2 / 3 / 4 / 5)
The student negotiates meaning (1 / 2 / 3 / 4 / 5)
The student conveys factual information (1 / 2 / 3 / 4 / 5)
The student gives personal opinions (1 / 2 / 3 / 4 / 5)
The student invites contributions from others (1 / 2 / 3 / 4 / 5)
The student agrees/disagrees appropriately (1 / 2 / 3 / 4 / 5)
The student changes topic appropriately (1 / 2 / 3 / 4 / 5)

ROBERT: How do you actually do this? I mean – how many students do you have in your class?

JUDY: Twenty at the moment.

ROBERT: So, how do you evaluate twenty students individually?

JUDY: Well, I have them working in groups of four. Over the course of a week, I sit in on each group – one group a day. It's quite manageable once you get used to the checklist and the procedure. After the class, I have an individual feedback session with each student.

KIT: And what do the students think?

JUDY: They really like it, because it gives them concrete and specific feedback. Without a checklist such as this, you end up giving vague and imprecise feedback, such as "You need to get more involved in the discussion." Next semester, I want to get the students to carry out their own evaluations. Every student will have a copy of the checklist, and, at the end of the task, I'll have a reflection session in which the students do their own self-evaluation.

VAN: That's kind of similar to the procedure I experimented with.

ROBERT: What was that?

VAN: I used production tasks – role-plays, information gap tasks, problem-solving tasks. Instead of using a checklist created by someone else, I got the students themselves to come up with the criteria for judging their performance. Then I evaluate the students. During the week, I have a schedule of students I'm going to observe. I assess three to four students each lesson, and then have a feedback session with them at the end of the class. I don't use a rating scale like Judy – I give them more global feedback. But I like Judy's idea of giving precise feedback.

ROBERT: I used a rather different procedure.

JUDY: What was that?

ROBERT: Well, I read an article about getting learners to keep reflective journals and learning logs, and I thought that maybe these could be used to assess learner language.

KIT: How did it work out?

ROBERT: Well, to start out it didn't work very well. They didn't really know what to write.

KIT: So what did you do?

ROBERT: I used a technique called guided journals. I gave the students sentence starters which they had to complete.

KIT: Like what?

ROBERT: Like "This week I studied . . .," "This week I learned . . .," "This week I used English in these places . . .," "This week, I spoke English with these people . . .," "This week I made these mistakes . . ."

KIT: And what happened?

ROBERT: It was really interesting. At the beginning of the semester, the learners just used single words and short phrases to complete the statements. "This week, I talked to my physics lecturer," that sort of thing. By the end of the semester, they were writing whole paragraphs. "This week I talked to a tourist at the ferry pier. She asked me how to buy tickets and I told her how to do it." So their written language was longer and more complex. The responses were also interesting. My not-so-hidden agenda was to get students to increase their language out of class. Just asking questions about out-of-class use prompted them to look for opportunities to use English out of class.

JUDY: How about you, Kit? What did you do?

KIT: I used a summative assessment task – learner portfolios.

ROBERT: Portfolios?

KIT: Yes, you know how artists, architects, graphic designers, and so on have port-folios of their work – basically samples of their best work. With our students, the portfolio will contain samples of their written and spoken work. At the beginning of the semester, I explained what a portfolio was, and what it should contain. I also gave them a sample to give them a clearer idea of what a portfolio was.

VAN: I'm not clear exactly what a portfolio might contain. Can you give me an example?

KIT: I told the students that the portfolio should start off with a self-introduction explaining what they had included and why. The body of the portfolio consists of samples of spoken and written language. They then have to provide evidence of growth and development.

ROBERT: How do they do that?

KIT: Well, they could put in the first draft of a written piece of work and then a second draft revised on the basis of feedback from the teacher, or an assignment written at the beginning of the semester, and another one written at the end. Again, with oral language, they can include a sample of their spoken language at the beginning of the semester, and another sample at the end.

JUDY: I was going to ask you how they submit samples of spoken language – DVD?

KIT: Oh, cooler than that. I get them to submit electronic portfolios – e-portfolios. They scan their written work, and can upload their spoken samples.

JUDY: Wow! Sounds complicated!

KIT: Actually it isn't. There are lots of free websites that make it pretty easy. If you're interested, check out this site. It's just an example, but it will give you an idea: http://elc.polyu.edu.hk/ecNews/1009/Spotlighton.htm.

Anyway, the final part of the portfolio is evidence of reflective learning. This is the most important part of the portfolio, in my opinion. It gives the learner an opportunity to describe their own strengths and weaknesses as a learner.

Commentary

The four assessment procedures described by these teachers are observation and feedback, production tasks, learner journals, and portfolios. Interestingly, all of these assessment procedures focus on assessment for learning, although the portfolio also involves assessment of learning. They are also all direct rather than indirect assessments. Also interesting was the fact that none of the teachers chose to use written quizzes of a traditional kind.

TASK

Select an assessment technique. Describe the technique. If possible, try it out with a group of students, and write a short report on the experience.

Summary

Content focus	Assessment
Vignette	Learner self-assessment
Issue in focus	Purposes for and timing of assessment
Key principles	1. When designing assessments, always begin with the objectives of the course. 2. Involve learners in the learning process. 3. Ensure that the assessment tool is appropriate to the purpose of the assessment. 4. Do not use assessments that have been carried out for one purpose for other purposes. 5. The ultimate judge of success is the interlocuter beyond the classroom
What teachers want to know	Direct versus indirect assessment
Small group discussion	Techniques for assessment

Further Reading

Carless, D., G. Joughin, and Ngar-Fun Liu (2006) *How Assessment Supports Learning*. Hong Kong: Hong Kong University Press.

This book is a collection of practical assessment tasks that exemplify the philosophy of assessment for learning described in this chapter. Two introductory chapters provide a clear rationale for learning-oriented assessment and present a conceptual framework for the approach. Although designed for students in higher education, many of the tasks can be modified for other contexts.

References

Brindley, G. (2003) Classroom-based assessment. In D. Nunan (ed.) *Practical English Language Teaching*. New York: McGraw-Hill.

Carless, D., G. Joughin, and Ngar-Fun Liu (2006) *How Assessment Supports Learning*. Hong Kong: Hong Kong University Press.

Ioannou-Georgiou, S. and P. Pavlou (2003) *Assessing Young Learners*. Oxford: Oxford University Press.

Nunan, D. (2004) *Task-based Language Teaching*. Cambridge: Cambridge University Press.

Wajnryb, R. (1992) *Classroom Observation Tasks*. Cambridge: Cambridge University Press.

GLOSSARY

accent: A distinctive form of pronunciation that marks the speaker as belonging to a particular country, geographical region, or social class.

accuracy: The extent to which a non-native speaker's pronunciation converges with that of a standard variety of a given language.

affective variables: Mental characteristics or qualities that reflect attitudes and emotions. Affective variables in language learning include motivation, anxiety, identity, intelligence, personality, and aptitude.

assessment: Tools, techniques, and procedures for determining what learners know and can do in relation to a particular knowledge domain.

audiolingualism: A language teaching method based on behaviorist psychology and structural linguistics. The core belief underlying the method is that language learning is a process of habit formation.

authenticity: In language teaching, there are various types of authenticity. The most frequently discussed types of authenticity are text authenticity and task authenticity. An authentic text is one that came about in the course of genuine communication, rather than being specifically written for the purposes of language teaching and learning. Task authenticity refers to the extent to which a pedagogical task reflects the kinds of things we do with language in the world outside the classroom.

autonomy: The capacity to take control of one's own learning.

background knowledge: The general and contextual knowledge we have on a particular subject.

bottom-up processing: Making sense of a sentence or utterance by starting with the smallest meaningful elements of language. In the case of spoken language, these are individual sounds, known as phonemes. In the case of written language, these are individual letters of the alphabet.

clarification request: A conversational strategy in which a participant in a conversation asks for a reformulation of an utterance to clarify the meaning.

classroom discourse: Classroom spoken language that displays characteristics that are rarely, if ever, evident in spoken language beyond the classroom. These include display questions and the evaluation of a speaker's grammar and pronunciation rather than the content of the utterance.

coherence: The extent to which the sentences and utterances in a stretch of spoken or written discourse make sense or 'hang together.'

cohesion: Linguistic devices that make explicit certain relationships in spoken and written language. For example, conjunctions such as 'and,' 'however,' 'although,' and 'next' signal various logical relationships.

collocation: Words that commonly co-occur such as 'mountainous waves.' Collocation also refers to words that are related by virtue of belonging to a particular semantic field. For example, animal, tiger, elephant, zebra, giraffe.

communicative activity: A classroom procedure that practices a particular linguistic feature such as a grammatical item which also has a meaning-focused outcomes.

communicative competence: The ability to communicate effectively by mobilizing grammatical, discoursal, strategic, and cultural knowledge.

communicative language teaching: A philosophical family of approaches to language teaching which emphasize language as a tool for communication rather than an abstract system of rules.

complexity: The existence in a learner's utterances of complex grammatical structures such as subordination and relativization.

comprehensible input: Spoken texts which, while they contain linguistic features that the learner doesn't understand, are comprehensible to the learner because of the context in which they occur. Stephen Krashen, in his Input Hypothesis, argued that comprehensible input provided the necessary and sufficient condition for language acquisition.

comprehensible output: The production of utterances by a speaker that are comprehensible to an interlocutor. Proponents of comprehensible output argue that while comprehensible input is necessary, it is not sufficient for acquisition. Comprehensible output is also required.

comprehension check: A conversational strategy in which the speaker checks to see whether the listener has correctly understood.

confirmation check: A conversational strategy in which the listener checks where he or she has correctly understood the speaker.

conscious learning: The deliberate effort to memorize and master a linguistic feature of the target language such as a new word, grammar point, pronunciation feature, or aspect of discourse.

contact assignments: An out-of-class activity requiring the learner to engage in an authentic interaction with one or more native speakers or fluent users of the target language.

contextual knowledge: Knowledge of variables associated with a communicative event such as the situation, the topic of the conversation, the relationships between the speakers taking part in a conversation, and the purpose of the conversation. Awareness of variables facilitates conversation.

contrastive analysis: The analysis of a feature of one language in comparison with another. When a feature, such as a system of definite and indefinite articles, is shared by both languages, it is assumed that learning that feature in the target language will be facilitated. When a feature is not shared, for example when the first language does not have articles but the target language does, that feature will be more difficult to learn. When the feature is shared but functions differently in the target language, learning will also be impeded.

contrastive rhetoric: Differences in discourse patterns between languages that reflect cultural differences.

corpus (pl. corpora): A large computerized body of words or texts that can be used to carry out different types of linguistic analysis that lead to the identification of patterns of use.

creative speaking: When learners achieve communicative goals by formulating their own utterances rather than memorizing and reproducing a dialogue provided by a teacher or a book, we say they are using the language creatively.

curriculum development: The complex process of creating a syllabus, identifying appropriate methodological tasks along with assessment and evaluation instruments, and integrating all of the procedures and instruments in the creation of courses and programs.

declarative knowledge: Knowledge that can be explicitly stated.

deductive teaching/learning: A teaching/learning procedure in which a teacher, textbook, or other source explains a rule or principle and then learners complete exercises to apply and consolidate the rule.

descriptive grammar: Descriptive grammars seek to describe and explain language as it is actually used by speakers.

dialect: A variety of language exhibiting grammatical features and vocabulary that differ from standard varieties of the language. Dialects, along with accents, often mark speakers as belonging to a particular geographical region or social class.

direct assessment: Assessment tasks in which the task mirrors the way that language is used for real communication in the world beyond the classroom.

discourse: A stretch of spoken or written language viewed within the communicative context in which it occurs.

discourse skills: The ability to make contributions to a conversation that are relevant and appropriate to the topic, the situation, preceding utterances, and the overall purpose of the conversation.

EAP: English for Academic Purposes. Students acquire skills such as listening to lectures, summarizing academic texts, taking part in tutorial discussions, and following the conventions of academic written genres.

eclectic method: A 'method' that draws on a range of other methods and approaches that fits the pedagogical context and the teacher style as well as learners' strategy preferences, rather than adhering rigidly to a set of prescriptive principles.

EFL: English as a Foreign Language. The teaching of English in countries where it is not one of the main languages of communication within the community. The distinction between English as a Foreign and English as a Second Language has become increasingly problematic with the spread of English as a global language.

email tandem exchange: An out-of-class technique in which two second language learners set up an email exchange. Each partner is learning the other's first language as their second language. They write to their partner in their second language, and receive a response in their partner's first language, which is their second language. They then comment on their partner's message, pointing out grammar and vocabulary mistakes and indicating how a first language speaker would have framed the message.

ESL: English as a Second Language. The teaching of English to speakers of other languages in contexts where English is the (or a) major medium of communication within the community.

ESP: English for Specific Purposes. Courses of study that prepare learners for specific communicative domains. These are usually related to occupations or areas of professional study such as Business English, Technical English, English for Law, English for Flight Attendants.

evaluation: The collection and analysis of data relating to courses or curricula designed to improve those courses or curricula by identifying those aspects that need to be improved, why they need to be improved, and how they might be improved.

exchange structure analysis: Originally developed by Sinclair and Coulthard (1975) for the description and analysis of classroom discourse. They began with the 'lesson' as the largest unit of analysis, and progressively broke this down into smaller units, in much the same way as grammarians break down sentences into small units such as clauses, phrases, words, and morphemes.

extensive reading: Doing lots of reading in the target language outside the classroom primarily for pleasure (rather than to study language). The focus is on becoming a fluent reader. Acquisition largely happens incidentally.

feedback: Information provided to the learner on their spoken and written language production. Feedback can be provided by the teacher, fellow students, or individuals outside of the classroom. (For example, non-comprehension by a native speaker is a form of feedback.) Feedback can be formal, for example, in the form of test results, or informal.

field: One of the three variables in Halliday's concept of register. Field refers to the content of the piece of spoken or written communication. In oral interactions, it answers the question; "What are the speakers talking about?"

fluency: The speed and intelligibility of spoken language. Fluency contrasts with accuracy.

formal grammars: Grammars that describe the underlying form of sentences or utterances without reference to their function.

formative assessment: Assessment carried out during a course. Formative assessment is designed to give feedback to the learners on strengths and weaknesses as the course progresses, rather than providing a final grade or report at the end of the course.

functional grammars: Grammars that seek to provide an explanation of grammatical forms in terms of their grammatical functions or purposes.

good language learners: The 'good' language learner is someone who achieves better than average levels of proficiency than other learners over a comparable period of time. Over the years, there has been considerable research into the factors that account for this superiority.

grammar dictation (also known as dictogloss): A technique designed to activate and consolidate learners' knowledge of a grammatical item or items. The teacher reads a short text containing target grammar items at near normal speed. Learners jot down the content words they hear, and then work collaboratively in small groups to share the words they wrote down, and reconstruct the original passage. In order to do this, they have to draw on their knowledge of the grammar items in the text.

grammar-translation: A method that dominated language teaching before the emergence of audiolingualism, communicative language teaching, and other approaches and methods that came along to challenge it. It involves the explicit analysis of target language grammar, along with exercises in translating sentences and texts back and forth between the first and target languages. The method remains popular today, and translation studies have made something of a comeback.

graphic organizers: Graphic organizers are also known as concept maps, mind maps, and also by various other names. They are graphical ways of showing the key concepts in a text or area of study as well as the relationship between these.

hypernym: The general word that covers a particular semantic field. For example, *furniture*, which is a hypernym of *chair*, *table*, *bed*, *wardrobe*, etc.

hyponym: Words belonging to a particular semantic field that are subordinate to a more general word. (For examples, see the entry above.)

indirect assessment: Assessment items and instruments that do not directly provide data on a learner's ability to use language communicatively. Multiple-choice, true/false, and fill-in-the-blank exercises are examples of indirect assessment items.

inductive teaching/learning: A teaching/learning procedure in which learners study sentences, texts, or other pieces of language data and derive a rule or principle which they articulate and then apply.

information gap tasks: Pedagogical tasks in which speakers have unequal access to information that has to be shared in order for the task to be completed successfully. In one-way tasks, one speaker has all the information and the other speaker or speakers have to obtain the information. In two-way tasks (which can include more than two speakers), the speakers all have different information that has to be shared for the task to be completed.

input hypothesis: Formulated by the linguist Stephen Krashen, the hypothesis states that we acquire a language when we understand messages in that language.

integrated skills: An approach to teaching/learning in which two or more of the four skills (listening, speaking, reading, and writing) are integrated rather than taught separately in lessons or units of work.

intensive reading: the detailed study of relatively short texts. In contrast with extensive reading, the goal of intensive reading is complete understanding.

interactional skills: Skills needed by speakers for the successful conduct of transactional and interpersonal conversations. These skills include topic selection, development, and change, speaker selection and change, getting a turn in a conversation and handing over the turn, the negotiation of meaning, keeping a conversation going, terminating a conversation, disagreeing politely, as well as many other functions that are needed for successfully carrying out a conversation.

interactive reading: An approach that gets readers using both bottom-up and top-down strategies in reading a text.

interpersonal speaking: Two major types of speaking are transactional speaking and interpersonal speaking. In interpersonal conversations, the main purpose is a social one, for example to initiate, develop, or maintain a friendship, rather than to obtain goods and services.

intonation: The upward or downward movement of voice pitch to convey different meanings. In some languages, the pitch movement signals differences in semantic meaning. In other languages, it signals differences of attitudinal and emotional meaning.

learner-centeredness: In a learner-centered classroom, learners are actively involved in making decisions about what to learn, how to learn, and how to be assessed. Additional, in the classroom, learners are active participants in skills development rather than passive recipients of knowledge.

learning goals: Curriculum goals that focus on learning processes rather than language content.

learning-how-to-learn: Classroom activities that are focused on learning processes. The aim of these activities is to develop the skills that learners need in order to make informed decisions about what they want to learn, how they want to learn, and how they want to be assessed. These are skills they need in order to become more active participants in their own learning.

learning strategies: The cognitive and communicated processes that learners use in order to acquire a language. Common language learning strategies include memorizing, repeating, inferencing, and predicting as well as inductive and deductive reasoning.

learning styles: Broad, general approaches to learning that are determined by a learner's cognitive makeup and personality.

lexical phrases: Set phrases in a language that occur frequently. These can be learned as formulaic chunks in the early stages of acquiring another language, and subsequently broken down by the learner.

lexis/lexicon: The total stock of words in a language.

listening strategies: Strategies needed for successful listening. Examples include listening for gist, listening for specific information, making inferences, using context, and utilizing background knowledge.

macroskills: The term macroskills refers to the four means of processing and producing language: listening, speaking, reading, and writing.

metacognitive tasks: Tasks that raise learners' awareness of the processes and strategies underlying learning.

metalanguage: Language about language, for example technical terms for describing pronunciation, vocabulary, grammar, and discourse.

method: A method is a prescriptive set of procedures that are based on beliefs about the nature of language and the learning process.

methodology: Principles and procedures for selecting, sequencing, and justifying learning tasks and activities.

methods debate: A debate over the best method for language teaching. The debate usually raged of the relative merits of two methods that were fashionable at any given time: grammar-translation versus audiolingualism, audiolingualism versus cognitive code learning and so on. The aim was to find the one best method. The methods debate began to fade as it was realized that there was no such thing as a 'best' method, and that all methods had good points and bad points.

minimal pair: Two words that differ in a single phoneme, resulting in differences in the meaning of the words. Example 'dip,' 'tip.'

mode: One of the three variables in Halliday's concept of register. Mode refers to the means of communication: whether it is spoken or written, face-to-face or mediated by technology – telephone, Skype, etc.

modes of classroom discourse: according to McCarthy and Walsh (2003), there are four basic modes of classroom discourse: managerial mode, materials mode, skills and systems mode, and classroom context mode.

negotiated learning: Learning in which content, procedures, and assessment are negotiated between teacher and learners.

negotiation of meaning: The interactional 'work' done by speakers and listeners to ensure successful and accurate communication. Speakers do things such as checking that the listener has correctly understood. Listeners repeat what they think they heard and take other measures to make sure that they have understood. It is hypothesized that when second language learners are speaking, these strategies facilitate language acquisition.

out-of-class learning: Learning that goes on out of the classroom. The learning can be blended with classroom learning or totally independent of the class-room. It can also be student self-directed, teacher-directed, or a collaboratively determined between teacher and student.

pedagogical tasks: Tasks that are designed for and enacted in the classroom. These tasks can be ranged on a continuum from those in which there is a direct relationship between the pedagogical tasks and an equivalent authentic out-of-class task at one end of the continuum and an indirect, tenuous rela-tionship at the other.

phoneme: The smallest meaningful unit of sound in a language.

phonics: An approach to the initial teaching of reading alphabetical languages by decoding words through a process of matching written symbols with their aural equivalents.

phonological skill: The ability to blend phonemes to form words. This variant on phonics is also known as synthetic phonics.

phonology: Study of the sounds of a particular language and the relationship between sounds and meaning in the language.

prescriptive grammar: Prescriptive grammars set out rules of 'correctness' speci-fying how grammar items should be used. There rules are sometimes at odds with the ways in which speakers actually use language.

procedural knowledge: Contrasts with declarative knowledge. Procedural knowl-edge is knowing how to do things. Declarative knowing is 'knowing that.' In language learning, for example, it is the ability to state a grammatical rule. Proce-dural knowledge is the ability to use the rule correctly and appropriately for communication. Some learners have declarative but not procedural knowledge. They can state a rule, but not use it effectively to communicate. Others have procedural but not declarative knowledge, that is, they can use a grammatical item but can't state the rule. First language speakers who are not linguists typically have procedural knowledge of their first language but not declarative knowledge.

productive skills: Refers to speaking and writing.

real-world tasks: Communicative tasks that are carried out in the world outside the classroom.

receptive skills: Refers to listening and reading.

reflective learning: Thinking about a learning task and self-evaluating one's per-formance. Making judgments about what one did well and how one can improve on one's performance.

register: An approach to the analysis of texts or conversations that attempts to explain textual variation in terms of three variables: field (what the text or conversations are about), tenor (the relationship between the participants in a conversation), and mode (the channel or vehicle of communication – whether spoken or written, face-to-face or telephone, etc.).

reliability: In language testing, this refers to consistency. If a test yields the same results when administered to the same student on different occasions, or if it yields the same results if scored by different markers, then it is deemed to be reliable.

repetition: Processing or producing the same language repeatedly. Repetition can be rote or can have a meaningful dimension. Meaningful repetition is deemed to be more effective for language learning.

reproductive speaking: Speaking tasks in which learners imitate and manipulate a model provided by the teacher or some electronic means.

rhythm: A suprasegmental feature of language. Rhythm is determined by the pattern of stressed and unstressed syllables in an utterance. Languages in which stressed and unstressed syllables alternate are called syllable timed languages. English is a stressed timed language. The length of an utterance is determined by the number of stressed syllables it contains.

role-play: In a role-play a learner has to play the part of a character other then themselves and solve a problem, come to a decision, argue a case, or complete some other similar task with a group of learners who will have different roles, and often different agendas.

scaffolding: Providing a supporting framework to facilitate a learning task or activity. For example, a listening task might be supported with a list of key vocabulary. A speaking task might be preceded by a model conversation that the learners rehearse.

schema building: Task and activities that build background knowledge of a topic or situation that the students are about to encounter in a task, lesson, or unit of work.

segmental phonology: The study of the phonemes in a language.

self-directed learning: Learning that is determined and carried out by the learner outside the classroom.

(The) Silent Way: A language teaching method popular in the 1970s that was based on principles of inductive learning. It was designed to force learners to develop their own inner resources for learning rather than relying on the teacher.

simulations: similar to role-play, except that learners act as themselves rather than adopting the role of another character.

speech function/speech act: The things we do with language. While there are many things we do with language, the pioneering speech act theorists Austin and Searle boiled these down to just five.

stress: A suprasegmental feature of language. The emphasis placed on syllables within a word and on words within sentences.

structural linguistics: The study of language as a set of sentence patterns.

subconscious acquisition: The notion that language acquisition occurs below the level of conscious awareness. The linguist Stephen Krashen proposed the controversial notion that subconscious acquisition and conscious learning were two separate cognitive processes, and that contrary to conventional belief, conscious learning did not 'turn into' acquisition.

Suggestopedia: An idiosyncratic method developed by Bulgarian psychologist Lozanov, who believed that the human mind was capable of performing prodigious feats of memory under the right conditions, specifically when in a relaxed, almost hypnotic, state. The root of the method was to have learners listen to the target language while simultaneously listening to Baroque music.

summative assessment: Assessment carried out at the end of a course, usually to provide a record of achievement or some form of certification.

suprasegmental phonology: The study of those features of pronunciation that convey attitudinal and emotional rather than semantic information. These features include stress, rhythm, and intonation among others.

syllabus design: The selection, sequencing, integrating, and justifying of content for a syllabus: content can include some or all of the following: pronunciation, grammar, vocabulary, topics, themes, situations, functions, and text types.

task-based language teaching: A family of procedures in which the 'task' is the basic building block of the instructional design.

task cycle: An instructional cycle including a pre-task, task, and follow-up.

teacher talk: The special register used by teachers in the classroom. Teacher talk includes discourse features that are not normally part of everyday speech such as display questions and evaluative feedback on student talk.

tenor: One of the three variables in Halliday's concept of register. Tenor refers to the relationship between participants in a communicative act. A conversation between two strangers will differ in certain ways from a conversation on the same topic between two family members.

TESOL: The Teaching of English to Speakers of Other Languages. The term refers both to the field as well as to the professional association of language teachers.

thematization: The process of giving prominence to a particular element within a sentence by placing it at the front of the sentence. The theme of the sentence "Jack joined the choir" is 'Jack.' In "The choir is what Jack joined" the theme is the choir.

top-down processing: The use of contextual and background knowledge to comprehend spoken and written texts.

Total Physical Response (TPR): A comprehension-based method of teaching in which the teacher gives a sequence of instructions to the learners in the imperative which the students have to carry out. The method can be used to practice a wide range of grammar and vocabulary.

transactional speaking: Conversations in which the main goal is to obtain goods or services rather than to socialize.

uptake: When a learner hears a new piece of language (for example, a grammar item or new word) used by someone else, such as a teacher or another student, and subsequently incorporates the item into his own speech, this is known as uptake.

validity: In language assessment, when an assessment item mirrors one of the goals of a course, we say that the item has validity.

word: 'Word' is one of the trickiest concepts in language to define. Most dictionaries define it as a single unit of meaning shown with a white space either side when written down. Like other definitions, there are problems with this one. (Contractions such as 'it's' 'they're,' and we've' fit the definition, but are actually two words, not one.) However, it's probably the closest we can come to a working definition.

word family: A group of words derived from a root word.

References

McCarthy, M. and S. Walsh (2003) Discourse. In D. Nunan (ed.) *Practical English Language Teaching.* New York: McGraw-Hill.

Sinclair, J. and M. Coulthard (1975) *Towards an Analysis of Discourse.* Oxford: Oxford University Press.

INDEX

Note: Page numbers in bold type (e.g. **174–5**) indicate detailed discussion of the topic.